Wine is...

The Perfect Blend of Intellectual Pursuit

...and Pure Hedonism

[Sign in the China Coast Winebar....Hong Kong]

Sonderho Press, Ottawa K2P 0V4
Copyright © 2016, Larry Horne
All rights reserved. Published 2016.

All photos copyright Larry Horne and Alice Bannon Horne with the following exceptions: page 14, copyright Derek Saunders, page 21 copyright Mariposa Folk Festival, page 30 copyright Richard Todd. The artwork on pages 16, 43 and 66 are copyright of their respective owners.

This book is the result of the author's independent research and has been created to provide accurate information concerning the subject matter. Although every precaution has been taken in the preparation of this book, the author and publisher assume no responsibility for errors and omissions.

No portion of this publication may be reproduced or transmitted in any form or by any means, electronic or mechanical, including photography, recording, or any information storage or retrieval system, without permission in writing from the publisher, except by a reviewer who may quote brief passages in a critical article or review to be printed in a magazine or newspaper, or electronically transmitted on radio, television, or the Internet.

Designed and published by **Sonderho Press**.
Edited by **Lesley Fraser**.

Printed in the United States of America.

ISBN: 978-0-9917484-6-4

This book is printed on acid-free paper.

Cover: Original artwork by **Alice Bannon Horne**

Besotted

My Love Affair with Wine

*To Janice
That teenage girl I knew
so long ago...*

Larry
Larry Horne

NOV 16

SONDERHO PRESS. OTTAWA

Dedication

To my lovely granddaughters, Emma, Evelyn, Penny, and Mavis.
And to my life partner of forty-four years, Alice Benz.

Alice in the Greenlane vineyard.

Contents

Foreword		c
Preface		e
Chapter 1	Tasting As an Excuse for Drinking	1
Chapter 2	Horne Brothers Fine Wines	7
Chapter 3	Calamus Estate Winery	15
Chapter 4	The Emerging Ontario Wine Industry Has Arrived	25
Chapter 5	Wine Collecting	31
Chapter 6	Diary of a Wine Tourist	35
	Napa / Sonoma	35
	New Zealand (Vines Mag excerpt)	37
	Australia	43
	Germany	49
	Alsace	51
	Champagne	52
	Switzerland	53
	Burgundy	54
	Tuscany	58
	Provence and Southern Rhône	60
	Finger Lakes	63
	Robbery on the High Seas	65
	New Zealand Revisited	68
	British Columbia	73
	Epilogue	75
Wine Hall of Fame		77
Acknowledgements		81

Foreword

By Robin Horne

This is a book about experience as seen through the eyes of Larry, a tale about paddling along life's river. This part of his river is all about the wine. Wine takes a hold on some people, and I'm not just talking about savouring and drinking the stuff. Larry has paddled his way through planting, growing, picking, vintning, selling, testing, sampling, evaluating, learning, sharing, pouring, recording, fretting, sweating, and investing in wine! You see, the wine just leaks into every step of Larry's voyage. I'm fortunate to have come along on a lot of this grand tour. You've probably seen me over the years, up in the bow, making repairs, bailing, navigating, and paddling madly all the while; Larry, planted in the stern, deftly directing our craft amidst the rocks and shoals, through some rough water, and into some pretty cool calm water. I digress ...

You're probably asking yourself, "Yes, but what has all this metaphoric paddling along rivers of wine have to do with Larry's life with wine?" The better question would be, "What has kayaking got to do with wine in a box?"

We've all seen bag-in-a-box wines in our local LCBO, stacked on the shelves in all their rectangular glory. Perhaps we might find a nice big box of Pinot Grigio front and centre on our own refrigerator shelf, its spigot ready to offer up a timely tipple or three. Larry and I used to

Kayaking in Georgian Bay in exchange for wine in a bag.

scratch our heads over wineries wasting such perfect packaging on bulk wine. "Why not put the good stuff in a bag? These boxes are smart, convenient containers that are great for larger quantities of wine. There is never any air space inside. As the bag collapses, it empties – and thus no nasty oxidation. Shame on those wine snobs who turn up their palates at such a grand contraption," we huffed while sagely nodding our heads at each other in agreement.

Such pontificating during Horne Brothers wine work often resulted in occasional over-filling of glass bottles on my part. Larry pressed home the odd double cork on his. Cursed be those bottles and corks! Years of bottling, imbibing, and pontificating followed, until a guided kayak trip cued a return visit of bag-in-a-box on Larry's river.

Larry does love boating, whether sailing in the Caribbean or on the Great Lakes, puttering around Wood Lake in the Granny boat, or braving rapids along the Muskoka River. After one particularly beautiful day kayaking among the breathtaking islands of Georgian Bay, Larry's outfitter/guide set up camp on some little island, then began to prepare the evening meal.

"Where's the wine?" Larry asked.

The saddened chef said that while he would love to serve his customers decent wine, he couldn't allow glass bottles on kayak trips. Tippy watercraft, rough water, rocky shores, and fine wine were, in his view, not a good fit. Then there was the problem of the clinking, rattling empties, which would have to be packed out. If only there was another way!

"Yes," said Larry, the wine light bulb switching on, "there is another way! Why don't I supply you with some hand-made Horne Brothers Fine Bag-o-Wine? We'll have it ready for you in time for the next paddling season."

"And what would you be wanting for a season's supply?" asked the now upbeat outfitter.

Larry took his family on a free overnight kayak trip the next season, where, of course, they all drank fine wine – from a bag.

Paddle on, Larry, paddle on!

Preface

"The whole process of living is enriched by the miracle that is wine."
– Alec Waugh

Like most people, I drank wine in my late teens and twenties with names like Mateus, Castelvetro, and, especially regrettably, Berrycup. There were probably a few Cold Ducks and Lonesome Charlies in there as well – all sweet, soft, and providing the requisite alcohol buzz.

On my first trip to Europe, in 1974, I revelled in how cheaply I could buy wine, the best example being Savin, a low-end Spanish product sold in plastic, refillable bottles for a few pesetas. My most-used phrase in France was *"Vin ordinaire, s'il vous plaît"* – the cheaper the better. But the real love affair didn't start until a decade later, when I was 36, on a return trip to Spain.

My wife, Alice, and I were travelling with our friends Tim and Lucie, and we became enamoured with Cava, Rioja, and, especially, a higher-end red called Torres Black Label. We rejoiced whenever we found it on a restaurant list or in a store. I purchased a bottle in Valencia to take to the island of Ibiza, packing it in my canvas duffel bag. On arrival at Ibiza Airport, a well-meaning Tim threw my bag off the carousel to the concrete floor. I can still hear the dull smash of glass and see the red liquid soaking through the bottom of the bag. That was the moment I realized how important a good bottle of wine had become to me.

e

The Horne brothers sampling early vintages of their wines.

That epiphany set off a voyage of discovery that would help define the next thirty years of my life, including extensive travel to the wine regions of the world.

After returning from Spain, I became a "collector," setting up a wine cellar in the basement of our house on Dault Road and eventually purchasing a wine cooler to house the more expensive reds. I also set up a manual system of recording and describing every wine that came into the house, in what is now a series of binders divided by region. To keep my new passion in check, I set a monthly budget, which has fluctuated over the years but rarely been ignored. I am now on the last page of that budget ledger started in 1986.

My brother, Robin, had been a long-time home winemaker, dating back to the 1970s, when he used to bootleg to my friends. I had dabbled in it (winemaking, not bootlegging) over the years, but in the late '80s we joined forces to form Horne Brothers Fine Wines, which led to buying barrels and tanks and leasing an acre of a Niagara vineyard.

In late 1988, I met Larry Cook at a dinner party. We both brought the same somewhat obscure Rhône wine and found we had many other things in common: same course at Ryerson, same family configuration, both working in advertising, not to mention sharing a name. By the end of the evening, we had resolved to start the Noble Rotters tasting club.

I also joined the Ontario Wine Society, which I am still an active member of, and sought out every wine show and tasting event I could to educate my palate. Regular visits, usually with Robin, to the fledgling Niagara wine region followed and eventually led to Alice and I moving there and me helping to start Calamus Estate Winery in 2005.

This is an attempt to preserve personal history, find a thread to tell some of my life story, and enjoy the reward of discovery as I recall the last thirty years of my life. A long-time friend who has written and published a book about his love affair with antiques asked me in the spring of 2015 "if I had a book in me." I said I thought I did. Here it is.

Noble Rotters at the Dault Road bar.

Tasting As an Excuse for Drinking

My wife, Alice, says that my whole life has been a wine tasting. I admit that whenever the opportunity arises, I love to compare wines: from the same grape, region, or vintage; same winemaker or vineyard but different years – it doesn't matter as long as there is a matchup and a winner.

I am not a sommelier, a wine expert, or, that dreaded term, wine connoisseur. I might accept "wine enthusiast" or "aficionado," and I think I have a pretty discerning palate. Developing that palate came from thirty years of wine tastings, especially "blind tastings," where you don't know what's in the glass – although there's often a frame of reference, such as "they are all Pinot Noirs" and you must determine their provenance. This can be the most humbling of endeavours, but it ensures that you are not drinking the label or the price tag; instead, you're letting your senses do the work. I do this almost every time Alice and I share a bottle of wine: I serve it to her blind (no, she doesn't wear a blindfold), and she has to guess the grape, maybe its origin and, of course, its cost. The key to success is figuring out what it's not. She has been a good sport about this and has become very good at identifying the wine; it's truly educational. I doubt I've ever had a bottle of wine with my brother (and there have been hundreds) when we haven't paired it up with something from his cellar and declared one of them superior or at least better value.

The forming of the Noble Rotters tasting club in January 1989 started with my desire to try a bottle of Vega Sicilia, the legendary Spanish red from the Ribera del Duero region. With a price tag of over $100, I was loath to pick one up for dinner that night and asked the consultant at what was then called the Rare Wine Store, on Queen's Quay, if it was worth the money. His name was Claudius Fehr (who eventually became one of Vintages' head purchasers), and he told me the obvious: "The only way to know that is to try it yourself." Sensing my resistance, he added, "Why not get some like-minded friends together, to share the cost? And better still, add in some other reds to give it perspective." And so was born the first Noble Rotters tasting.

A January afternoon at Grano.

I had met Larry Cook a month earlier at a dinner party, to which we both brought the same rather obscure Rhône red. We talked a lot about wine that night, and I presented him with my idea of starting a regular tasting club. He was keen to help, and we brought in two other charter members: Tim Arkell, who had shared my wine epiphany on our 1984 trip to Spain, and Jim Nelles, a co-worker at Western Broadcast Sales. I had first got to know Jim when we cut out of work early one Friday to go to a food-and-wine show out near the airport.

On a cold January night, the four of us met at the bar Robin and I had built in the back of our Dault Road house. That bar would become the home for the majority of Noble Rotter tastings over the next fifteen years.

We agreed on a threefold purpose for the club: to taste wines not usually affordable to us as individuals; to increase our wine knowledge and expand our palates through discussion and blind tasting; and to provide a forum for information and exchange on recent finds, bargains, and other wine news.

Remember, this was pre-internet and -email, so a face-to-face exchange was important. In fact, the minutes of the founding meeting were sent out by fax. We agreed to take turns organizing the tastings and providing the wine, cheese, and bread. Jim suggested the name Noble Rotters, a play on the word for the Botrytis mould that can enhance the flavour and sweetness of some white dessert wines. Alice designed a logo, and we were off and running – for 128 tastings, as it turned out. We agreed to meet at least six times a year, usually on a Thursday night. A year later, brother Robin joined the group, and in year three, Dom DiClemente, the husband of a co-worker, joined.

Blind tastings are among the most humbling of experiences. When one of us scored five out of five, it was a badge of honour, never to be forgotten, validating our imagined expertise. We always had five wines: four that fit the theme of the evening and one that didn't – the ringer. At one gathering, Dom suggested we use sparkling wine as a palate cleanser between wines. It actually works, but sparkling water would have been a more prudent choice.

On more than one occasion, our wine cellars were bet and lost, so sure we were of a wine's identity. Like a poker game where the stakes get wildly out of control, no one was ever forced to pay up.

The tastings made us more confident and savvy consumers. Dom and I once sent back three consecutive bottles at the old Hop 'n' Grape wine bar on College Street. Steam was coming out of the manager's ears (they were all expensive), but when two knowledgeable people both found the wines faulty, it had to be done. There are many older, expensive, and defective wines lurking in restaurant cellars, but most people, insecure in their wine expertise, drink them and pay up.

Like a rock band, there were personnel changes to the Rotters over the years. Tim dropped out after six years, replaced by Larry's sister, Lisa; a couple of years later, she gave way to Derek Saunders, whom I had met at a CBC tasting group. In 1997, we began to have annual al fresco tastings with spouses in various backyards and, eventually, at the Calamus Estate vineyards in Niagara. One of the most memorable there was a wine scavenger hunt. We divided into teams, each assigned a section of Niagara wine country, and set out to visit wineries and purchase bottles best suited for the multi-course meal that would follow back at the vineyard. It was great fun sourcing the wines and then unveiling (and drinking) our finds at an outdoor repast that would last several hours and culminate with music around a campfire, a Horne family tradition.

Another annual tradition, with eight or nine of us, was a tasting with a multi-course meal at Grano restaurant in Toronto. Dom knew the owner, Roberto, and he let us use a private room, usually on a Saturday afternoon in January. We even had our own waiter, Tom. He would pour each bottle of wine, usually ten to twelve of them in total, and then serve the next food course. What a hedonistic way to start the new year. We had many fabulous gatherings there, starting with a millennium tasting in 2000, our hundredth tasting in April 2004, and ending, fittingly, with an Italian tasting in 2008.

In 2009, we moved our tradition to Café Taste in Parkdale. The owner, Jeremy Day, a wine geek and entrepreneur, had become an early and loyal Calamus customer of mine. It was a smooth transition, but by then the Noble Rotters were losing steam, and over the next three years, our only tastings were the Café Taste gathering and a summer get-together around Robin's pool. In 2012, Jeremy sold the café and Robin filled in his pool; it was over after 23 years.

The Saturday afternoon delights were not done blind but, like all Rotter tastings, were accompanied by an information package on the wines and a tally sheet, on which each wine was scored out of 100 and we recorded our comments. I still have all 128 of these in several binders in my wine cellar, the complete history of the Noble Rotters and the thousand-plus wines tasted.

Of course, there were many other "tasting experiences." My friend John Brosseau introduced me to Nico van Duyvenbode, an Ottawa wine collector, writer, and renowned taster who sometimes purchased the contents of wealthy British collectors' cellars, including older vintages of Bordeaux, Burgundy, and Rhône wines.

Nico would hold monthly Saturday tastings at a lakefront high-rise in Toronto. The mid-morning gatherings ensured a fresh palate. The wines, usually two decades or more old, were always opened the night before and tasted twice, first without food and then with. It was there I discovered that red Bordeaux is meant to be consumed with a meal but red Burgundy can be enjoyed anytime. These tastings were intimate, never more than six people, and I learned a great deal, both from Nico and from the other participants.

Such was Nico's collection that I was able to purchase a birth-year wine, a 1950 Château Talbot, for my friend Tim's fortieth birthday. Nico's favourite château was Palmer, which gave me the idea to buy birth-year Palmers for my two sons to have on their sixteenth birthdays. Sadly, 1978 and 1981 were not great Bordeaux vintages, but they were enjoyed immensely just the same, at least by me.

At one time, there were three wine shows a year in the Toronto area, and I was a regular visitor to all of them. The first one I remember was in 1984 at the Coliseum at Exhibition Place. The show was the domain of all the big import agencies, Inniskillin being the sole Ontario exhibitor. As time went on, more and more Ontario wineries got involved, and we started to meet people like Jim Warren, of Stoney Ridge, and the Speck boys, who still run Henry of Pelham today.

In the late 1990s, at one of these shows, I met Chris Waters and Walter Sendzik, two young men who had started a wine magazine called *Vines*. After a long chat with both of them, I decided to subscribe, thinking the publication probably wouldn't last a year. Although I already subscribed to *Wine Tidings*, *Wine Access*, and the *Wine Spectator*, I thought I would like to support these amicable entrepreneurs. In 2005, I convinced Chris to buy a story about my trip to New Zealand (I've included it in the wine travels chapter). He wrote the first review of a Calamus wine in a 2006 column in the *St. Catharines Standard*, and I took the wine appreciation course that he still teaches at Brock University. Today, Chris continues to be the editor of *Vines*, now owned by Postmedia, and Walter is the mayor of St. Catharines.

A "day in Provence" in the Dault Road backyard.

Tasting wine at these shows for over twenty-five years developed my palate, introduced me to many industry stalwarts, and, especially the tutored tastings, increased my wine knowledge immensely.

I shouldn't leave out wine bars when it comes to palate education. Toronto's first was a place called Vines on Wellington Street East, and I still miss it. On one lunchtime visit, Larry Cook and I tasted all three single-vineyard Guigal Côtes du Rhône reds: La Landonne, La Mouline, and La Turque, affectionately known as the La Las. All three sell for over $400 a bottle now, so are out of reach even for a tasting portion.

Other old favourites include Jamie Kennedy's (now the Wine Bar) on Church, Crush on King West, Le Select Bistro, especially when it was on Queen West, and the late, great Hop 'n' Grape at College and Yonge. All of these places had good by-the-glass selections, allowing you to do your own comparisons and decide what to purchase a bottle of.

Classic wine bars like these seem to be a rarity now. St. Catharines doesn't have one anymore, although Treadwell, now in Niagara-on-the-Lake, qualifies. Allen's, on the Danforth, has probably the best selection of Ontario wine by the glass in Toronto, and C'est What, primarily a craft beer destination on Front Street, has a good VQA selection and a cozy pub atmosphere.

When you add in twenty years of Ontario Wine Society tastings, the Broadcast Society Vintners Club, every winery I've ever visited, twenty-five years of making wine, all those blending tastings at Calamus, tastings on board cruise ships and around kitchen tables, maybe my wife is right – just don't tell her.

Robin and Larry with Horne Brothers plaque and a bottle of "Best of Show" wine.

Horne Brothers Fine Wines

I had my first taste of homemade wine when my next-door neighbour brought over a bottle of dandelion wine. We were fifteen years old, I was babysitting my siblings on New Year's Eve, and I was desperate to try some "forbidden fruit." It tasted every bit as bad as it sounds, not fit for even teenage consumption. My next experience was even worse: I found a bottle left for my parents by another neighbour, Second World War veteran Walter Kosh. It was godawful, truly undrinkable, but try it I did. It sent me reeling and retching in that order. Fortunately, it didn't put me off wine for life.

You can make wine from just about any organic entity, and some of my early efforts reflected that: rosehips, peaches, pears from our backyard tree at Woodfield Road, to name a few. These were far superior to Kosh's wine, but I wanted more, and the next step was to buy concentrate, or a "wine kit" as they are commonly called. Concentrate from various grape varietals can be bought, along with all the required glass containers, siphons, and chemicals, at a local winemaking store. These days, most people make their wine at the store and just come to bottle it, but that wasn't good enough for me.

I made my first in-house wine in 1976, while living in Moncton, New Brunswick. It was a "French rosé," and my notes from the day describe it as "cloudy," a common fault in wines made by inexperienced winemakers. For the next fifteen years, I made a wine every year, at six different addresses, from all manner of sources. Only a couple were memorable for the right reasons.

My brother, Robin, had been making wine even longer and with more success. We decided to join forces to form Horne Brothers Fine Wines. Robin was the lead winemaker, and I was the palate, marketer, and cellar rat. Our first vintage was 1990, a Gewürztraminer and a Riesling from grape juice purchased from Jim Warren's fledgling Niagara winery, Stoney Ridge Cellars. Over the years, Jim continued to be a winemaking mentor to Robin and was helpful and supportive to me in the early years of Calamus.

The next year, we made eight different wines, and we were on our way to twenty-five years of successful wine production. We designed labels, brochures with price lists, and business cards, ignoring the fact that it was all illegal. Alice made our first labels by hand in Letraset. As the computer age dawned, we spent countless hours designing labels for each new vintage and wine.

In our brochure, we gave our *raison d'être*: to make wine that was superior to anything produced commercially at the same price. "Handmade wine, not homemade wine" was our motto. To that end, we invested in small oak barrels, glassware of all sizes, a corker, and a filter pump. We painstakingly removed labels from all the commercial wines we bought to bottle our own wine for the first fifteen years.

We had an early payoff when Robin's 1994 red blend won Best of Show at the Paris Fair wine competition. Sure it was Paris, Ontario, but there are plenty of good amateur winemakers out there, and this was a feather in our cap.

Original Horne Brothers label and history.

There was a story behind the origins of this wine. The crush came from Jim Warren, who supplied a lot of amateur winemakers back then – a source of conflict with his grape-growing partner of the time. Robin was late picking it up – space is always an issue at harvest – and was admonished by Jim, who had been forced to pull those pails out of cold storage and add yeast. By the time Robin showed up to take delivery, fermentation was well under way, foam bubbling up around the loose-fitting lids. You would have to say we got an assist from Ontario's most decorated amateur winemaker.

A six-pack of Horne Brothers wines.

The following year, we began to also source grapes from Lailey Vineyards, on the Niagara Parkway. David and Donna Lailey had been growing grapes there since 1970 and had opened a winery with winemaker Derek Barnett in 2001. The original vineyard was mostly French hybrids, and we had a go with most of them: Marechal Foch, Zweigelt, Baco Noir, Villard, de Chaunac, often blending with vinifera like Cabernet Sauvignon and Merlot. For whites, it was Seyval Blanc, Vidal, Kerner, and Auxerrois.

We made only small quantities of each, four to six cases, but production grew as we began selling to friends and relatives and became the wine provider for all manner of milestones and events. Everything from family weddings, anniversary parties, and special birthdays to bar mitzvahs and private parties had Horne Brothers wines. Our sales pitch was "We don't pay tax and neither do you." Speaking of the underground economy, I have traded wine for legal services, storage space, wine bottles, pharmaceutical drugs, artwork and photos for labels, a guitar tune-up, a birthday-party chef, football tickets, computer work, honey, a tape deck, a soundman, and weed.

I even supplied a kayak outfitter with plastic bags of wine for a couple of seasons in exchange for an overnight family kayak trip in Georgian Bay. Not surprisingly, I traded wine to get the plastic bags: from my brother-in-law, who owned a plastics business and supplied bags to a company that sold bag-in-a-box wine to the SAQ in Quebec.

I also managed to give away several cases of wine each year for all manner of events and occasions. I even gave one to a tow truck driver once. In the fall of 1998, Alice and I were returning from Brantford after a weekend of bottling

Robin and Derek putting up vineyard wires.

wine. Another driver hit us from behind on the Gardiner Expressway at over eighty kilometres per hour, totalling our vehicle and shaking us up considerably. Tow truck drivers are always the first on the scene at these accidents, and we were informed that we would need a flatbed. Waiting for it to arrive, the driver was about to light up a smoke when a policeman at the scene stepped into him about his carelessness; you see, there was liquid running out of the trunk of the car, and the cop thought it was gasoline. We, of course, knew it was our just-bottled Baco Noir. The driver had been good to us, and we rode in his cab to the wrecker's compound, where I presented him with a surviving bottle as a thank-you.

Toward the end of the 1990s, we started to shift our focus to varietals like Cabernet Sauvignon, Merlot, Chardonnay, Pinot Gris, and Gewürztraminer. Many of the grapes came from another iconic Niagara vineyard, Watson's, first purchased from the grape-pioneering father, John, and later from his son Kevin. We returned to buy juice there recently, after a twelve-year absence. It's still a family business, with a third generation now involved in the operation, and still cash only.

Around this time I met Derek Saunders at a wine tasting in the CBC Broadcasting Centre, where we both worked. Another CBCer and fellow oenophile, René Bertrand, and I had started a monthly wine tasting club called the Broadcast Society Vintners Club. René organized the wine and food, and I conducted the tastings. Derek came to the first gathering, and I quickly learned that he had a plan to plant a vineyard in Niagara and eventually start a winery; he was also an amateur winemaker. It was the beginning of a long and "fruitful" relationship that started with us working on a lease of 10 percent of a piece of land that Derek was purchasing near Beamsville. Eventually, after much lawyering, an agreement was reached on a ten-year lease, commencing January 1, 2000. We had no idea what turning a 10-acre fruit orchard into a vineyard entailed, but we soon found out – lots of money.

The land had to be cleared, then levelled and shaped, and tile drainage put in. Vines had to be purchased and planted, posts and wires had to be installed ¬– and that was just the beginning. We all had full-time jobs far from Niagara but spent what time we could trying to do some of it ourselves. This did not always work out. One year we rented a power, but hand-held, auger to put in the posts that would hold the wires at the end of each row. After a day of backbreaking work and only a few posts in place, we agreed that we now understood the origins of the phrase "It doesn't auger well." It was days like that I thought of the gift my mother had given me the previous Christmas, a book called *A Fool and Forty Acres*.

The Horne Brothers rows consisted of six hundred Chardonnay vines and three hundred each of Cabernet Sauvignon and Merlot. We would have no appreciable harvest for five long years.

Meanwhile, there was still wine to be made, and we wanted to start making it from fruit sourced from the Twenty Mile Bench, similar to what our vineyard would produce. Ed Gurinskas was an Ottawa resident who spent his weekends and holidays at his Cherry Street vineyard and Lakeview Cellars winery, which he had started in 1991. Eddie had also been an amateur winemaker and became our third supplier, but only of the same vinifera grapes that would eventually be grown at the Greenlane vineyard.

A harvest lunch after a morning of hand picking, Vince, second from left.

At this point, we were making a dozen different wines a year, including rosé, a dessert wine, and a Port-style wine, made from a "secret family recipe" not handed down from generation to generation. Our house blends were called Wood Lake white and red, a nod to the location of a family cottage that had to be sold that year. We even did a label commemorating the one-hundredth birthday of our hockey-playing great uncle, George Horne.

We had now built up a cellar of ten vintages, and that would continue for another fifteen years. One goal was to be able to go back and have multi-year tastings of the same grape, which we did many times. Some of the "library wines" from the last ten years still exist, and it's always interesting to pull one out to see how it's evolved ... or not.

In 2004, our vines finally started to produce, and we began a harvest tradition of inviting friends to pick, crush, and de-stem grapes. Often four Saturdays were devoted to this undertaking each fall. We would pick in the morning, provide a "farm lunch" with plenty of wine, and crush and de-stem in the afternoon. Robin, a real MacGyver, devised a unique hand method to do this messy task. You were rewarded with a finished bottle if you came back the next year. Many did, but none with the dedication of Robin's friend Vince, who was there for eleven consecutive years. We used a wooden grape press that Vince's father had brought over from Italy right up to our last harvest, which was in 2014.

After our lease with Derek expired in 2009, we continued the harvest tradition with our single row of Baco Noir, which had been moved from Robin's

Robin's unique crush and destemming system (2009).

Horne Bros *garagistes* at work in Brantford.

backyard to Greenlane to the Calamus vineyard. Those vines were ripped out in 2015.

We had only five harvests from the Greenlane vineyard. We had a lot of fun and drank a lot of wine that we had grown, but I don't know how anyone makes a living growing grapes. I looked at it as ten years of a golf club membership. I don't golf.

During those five years, we had to expand our facilities to accommodate some large harvests. Robin's garage was bursting at the seams with new stainless steel tanks, three 225-litre French oak barrels, and countless demijohns and carboys. Our full bottle inventory grew to the point that it had to be stored offsite, and I think we have a lifetime supply of Baco Noir.

It was twenty-five tremendously satisfying years working with my brother to craft some memorable wines, blending, racking, filtering, adding some "winemakers' secrets," bottling, designing labels, and tasting our way through what must be two hundred wines of various vintages and grapes.

I wrote down the story on every one of those wines: harvest dates and weather for the different grapes, sugar levels in the grapes, the size of the harvest, and who was there to help pick. The memories will continue until the last bottle's gone – or we are.

Calamus barn when purchased in 2001.

Calamus Estate Winery

In 2005, I left the broadcast industry after thirty years, we sold our house in Toronto's east end, and we moved to St. Catharines. I had long wanted a second career in a new location and now had the opportunity to invest in and help start a winery. The owners, Derek Saunders and Pat Latin, had planted two vineyards and had begun to renovate two nineteenth-century barns to house their venture. They wanted me to be sales manager of the yet-to-be-opened Calamus Estate Winery, just outside Jordan, Ontario.

I had a lifetime of experience in sales. My first sales job was selling my beekeeper father's honey door to door on our street when I was twelve. I also had a paper route, and collecting is an integral part of sales, as in "the sale isn't made until the bill is paid."

After my second year in the Radio and Television Arts program at Ryerson, I landed a unique summer job, selling Zip barbecue starter to non-chain retailers all over Ontario.

Zip was a solid cube starter that was used to start briquettes or charcoal when hibachis were popular, before electric starters and before gas barbecues took over as the grill of choice. I still use Zip today to start my wood fireplace. My job was to sell a product that most people had never heard of, from someone they had never seen before, asking for cash for the cartons I carried in the trunk of my car. Up to fifteen cold calls a day, every day, no repeat customers. I did fairly well, but it was the ultimate school-of-hard-knocks sales training.

Three years later, that summer job got me a full-time job selling airtime for Atlantic Television out of Moncton, New Brunswick. The old-school sales manager who hired me disregarded all my meager qualifications, including my recent RTA diploma, and said, "Anyone who made fifteen cold calls a day, I want on my sales force."

I was given the rookie territory of the North Shore of New Brunswick, which no one else wanted. Problem was, that was the only area of the province still receiving a black and white signal, and my potential clients were not happy with me or the station. To boot, I was an "Upper Canadian," probably taking a job from an out-of-work Maritimer. I could offer only slide commercials, no video, but at least they were in colour, which would stand out against the black and white programs, or so I claimed. It was even tougher than the Zip job, but I persevered. Within two years, I became the sales manager, and that led to a thirty-year career in broadcast sales.

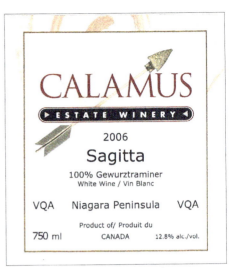

Original Calamus label (2006). They are now on their third version.

None of this prepared me for being the sales manager and, initially, the sole salesperson for Calamus Estate, which I helped get off the ground in 2006. Every sales call was cold, I was new to the area and the industry, and phone calls and emails were seldom returned. To make matters worse, the name was awkward and the label looked like it had been done at the last minute by amateurs, which it was.

The good news, and what kept me going in the very tough first two years, was that the wine was very good and well priced. Arthur Harder makes excellent wine.

The owners, Pat Latin and Derek Saunders, both lived and worked in Toronto, commuting to the winery whenever they could. It was left to me to do most of the promotion, marketing, contact with wine writers, and press releases in those early days. Most importantly, I had to make sales so there was some money coming in after seven years of it going out, including the modest investment I had made to help buy equipment, plant and maintain vineyards, and build a tasting and production facility.

Within a few months, I had our wine featured at On the Twenty restaurant, Gallery Grill at Hart House, Jamie Kennedy Wine Bar, Crush wine bar, Stone Road Grille, Treadwell, Zooma Zooma, and the Toronto Hunt Club – an impressive list but just the beginning. I never went anywhere out of Niagara without making a sales call and soon had customers in Stratford, Brantford, Barrie, and Guelph. By 2007, Calamus was in more than seventy restaurants, and I had several repeat and fairly loyal buyers.

One of those loyal customers was Jeremy Day, who owned Café Taste in Toronto's Parkdale neighbourhood and was a huge supporter of Ontario wine. With my inspiration, Jeremy ran the Ontario Wine Fair for six years. It featured eighteen Ontario wineries, fifteen cheesemakers, a multi-page program, and the People's Choice Awards. We also held the first offsite Calamus "futures tasting" there, which has become a winery fixture after every great Ontario red vintage. Unfortunately, Jeremy sold the café in 2012.

In 2007, Sheila Minkhorst joined Calamus as both an investor and as director of marketing. I had met Sheila after joining the Niagara chapter of the Ontario Wine Society and put her in touch with Pat and Derek. A deal was soon struck, and Sheila brought endless enthusiasm, lots of fresh ideas, and superb business acumen to the table.

One of the first projects that Sheila and I worked on together was *The Pressure Cooker*, a nine-part reality TV series about competing teams of chefs in a *Survivor*-type situation. After six gruelling days and nights of various rounds of cooking and harsh judgments from a panel of celebrity chefs, one team would emerge victorious. Each segment was sponsored by a Niagara winery, which included pairings of their wine with the finished meals and a chance for a winery principal to address the TV audience. After listening to producer Alan Aylward's pitch, Sheila and I signed Calamus on for the first episode.

I had gotten to know Alan when he was producing a groundbreaking TV series called *The New World Wine Tour*, which had taken him and his film crew

Derek with the first bottle off the line (June 2006).

to Niagara, California, BC, and France. His co-producer and host, Jonathan Welsh, was a veteran of Canadian stage and screen and, most impressive to me, was one of the original cast members of Hair, which I had attended on my twenty-first birthday.

Jonathan, aka Johnny Bordeaux (or whatever region they were in), was heard to say after 130 episodes – and wine intake beyond even my imagination – "I still haven't found a good breakfast wine." My favourite was a two-part interview he did with Robert Mondavi, then approaching ninety, and his wife. When asked about his wine consumption, Mondavi intoned, "A bottle for dinner, a half bottle for lunch; one day Mondavi wine, the next, somebody else's." Sitting outside at his Napa Valley estate, it sounded like the secret to a long, happy life.

Alan had also been very helpful to me, on my arrival in Niagara, by connecting me to the industry through people like Paul Speck, president of Henry of Pelham winery, and sending some sales leads my way.

September 15, 2008, must have been a slow news day. Derek, Sheila, and I found ourselves on the front page of the *St. Catharines Standard* with the header "Grape Expectations." It was a story on how the Niagara wine industry had nowhere to sell its wine but at the winery, to restaurants, and through the LCBO, which offered very limited shelf space at the time. The Wine Council of Ontario was asking for VQA (100 percent grown and bottled in Ontario) wine stores similar to those allowed in B.C.

As anyone knows who has bought wine outside Ontario, our system is among the most restrictive in the world. To make matters worse, the two largest wine companies in the country, one of them owned by US-based Constellation Brands, already had 240 wine kiosks in Ontario grocery stores. Many of the products sold there were foreign wines, usually imported in bulk and bottled here, so not VQA. Small and even medium-sized wineries were shut out, and we railed against the unfairness of this every chance we got, in the media, to provincial cabinet ministers, to customers, and to anyone who would listen. Market access, as we called it, was slow to come, first with expanded LCBO shelf space, then at farmers' markets, and, I'm pleased to say, finally in the province's supermarkets in 2016, eight years after that headline.

I've always been amazed at how "un-proud" many Ontario consumers and institutions are of the world-class wine being made here. This is not wine to be ashamed of, as maybe it was thirty years ago, but should have an exalted place among Ontario agricultural products.

I remember going to Ontario Place, a heavily subsidized showcase of Ontario to visitors from around the world, and being unable to find even one bottle of Ontario wine in any of its restaurants or bars. After some digging, I learned that an exclusive contract had been given to E & J Gallo Winery of Modesto, California. Some not-so-subtle emails copying a few sympathetic MLAs got some token VQA wines into Ontario Place's flagship restaurant.

Another outrage to me was attending the Mariposa Folk Festival, "an Ontario tradition for 50 years," its website proclaimed, to find that all the wine came from Chile. My emails to the directors are still unanswered. On a recent trip to Orillia I was pleased to learn they now serve Muskoka Craft beer and Niagara wines, progress is being made.

Arthur Harder working on his first Calamus vintage.

Even today, there are countless Ontario restaurants without a single VQA wine. As a salesperson I was often told, "Customers don't ask for them." If I was unable to sell them Calamus, I would suggest a bigger Ontario winery with better brand recognition. Fred Couch, of the Ontario Wine Society, came up with a card that I still use to this day: "It was a great meal but would have been better with some VQA wine." I don't know if it helps, but as a New York cabbie once told me, when I asked about his constant horn honking in Manhattan traffic, "it sure as fuck makes me feel better."

In June 2007, I agreed to start selling wines from nearby Kacaba Vineyards. At this point, I had established the Calamus brand and needed to become more efficient with my sales calls, especially when travelling outside of Niagara. So I took on another hard-to-pronounce name with another label no one liked.

John Tummon was a veteran and talented winemaker, so I was already partial to the product. Generally, Kacaba wines were a little more expensive and released later than Calamus wines, and they made wine from varietals that Calamus didn't, like Syrah and Pinot Noir. In this way I was able to offer my customers some variation in vintage, price, and grape type. When one winery ran out of, say, unoaked Chardonnay, I would start selling one from the other winery. It also meant I could make a little more money.

Ah yes, money from the wine business. Most of the sayings are true: "To make a small fortune, start with a large one," or "I didn't get into this for money; it's a labour of love." Having another source of income (mine was early pensions), a spouse who works (thank you, Alice), and being debt-free are all good ideas if you are thinking of selling wine for a living.

The people who operate most of Niagara's one-hundred-plus wineries mostly come from four backgrounds. There are the grape growers, usually multigenerational on the land, who got fed up selling their fruit to large wineries and decided they could make more money producing and selling the wine themselves. There are many of these, but Daniel Lenko, Lailey, and Sue-Ann Staff come to mind.

There are the corporate owners, like Constellation or Peller, which between them own Trius, Inniskillin, Thirty Bench, Jackson-Triggs, and others, as well as wineries around the world. Recently, Asian interests have been buying up Niagara wineries, including Marynissen and Alvento. I expect there will be many more sales to come in the quest for new sources of Icewine and other fine wines to satisfy the world's largest market. (Niagara isn't the only region affected by this phenomenon: in Bordeaux, for instance, Chinese investors have recently bought several châteaux.)

Then there are the entrepreneurs who have made money in other industries but have a passion for wine. Instead of racehorses or car collections, they've invested in vineyards and wineries. Michael Kacaba is a Bay Street lawyer, Martin Malivoire was in the film business, and Bob McCown, who recently bought Stoney Ridge, is a Toronto sportscaster. "Celebrity labels" are a subset of this category: Wayne Gretzky, Mike Weir, and Dan Aykroyd. In the US, you'll find Barbra Streisand's, Drew Barrymore's, and Arnold Palmer's names on labels. These people have little or nothing to do with the actual wine; rather, they're vanity projects wherein they're paid for the use of their names and usually some marketing and promotion. In a few cases, like that of Mike Weir Winery, some of the revenue goes to charity.

Alice and me at Mariposa in 2010 with the Six String Nation guitar.

The last and most challenged group are those who have no alternate wealth source, didn't inherit or grow up on vineyards, are not winemakers, and haven't been bought by a big corporation. Pat and Derek at Calamus are part of this group. They work one-hundred-hour weeks, rarely take a vacation, and constantly are convincing some bank why they should lend them more money. These people can make a stress-filled living, enjoy a lifestyle to a certain extent, but they'll have no real monetary gain until the day the business is sold.

People used to refer to me as "retiring to the wine business," which I found laughable. I was working twice as many hours for a quarter of the pay compared to my media-rep career. But I had been doing some variation of that for thirty years, and it's hard to stay excited about five-second video billboards and "brought to you bys." The wine business was an enormously challenging start-up from virtually nothing, and it provided me, at fifty-seven, a new life chapter in a new location. It was the best move I had made since leaving my six-figure job in 1985 for three months on the road with two kids and a trailer – equally irrational, but immensely satisfying.

Suffice to say that selling Niagara wine to restaurants was the biggest sales challenge of my life. I had come from a business (national television ad sales) where people employed at ad agencies would call and ask you to submit proposals, with about a 75 percent success rate; in the restaurant industry, few people ever called you back. Persistence and a good product at a reasonable price were my only allies. If I managed an initial sale, my success rate for a follow-up was less than 50 percent, and the effort-to-sales ratio was enormous. In TV land, I was used to million-dollar deals; in the world of small wineries, $2,000 was a big hit. To add to the challenge, restaurants, unlike large ad agencies, have a high bankruptcy rate, and we were stung more than once on unpaid invoices.

A few wonderful customers, like Steve del Col, who ran Zooma Zooma Café in Jordan, would give us a credit card to keep on file, so we never worried about getting paid. Steve and his wife, Jacqueline, were a joy to deal with. I always said, "If they were all like them, I'd still be selling wine."

Another treat to deal with was James Treadwell, the sommelier and part owner with his father, Stephen, of Treadwell Cuisine. Located in Port Dalhousie for many years and now in Niagara-on-the-Lake, Treadwell is, in my opinion, Niagara's best restaurant. James had every wine rep in the region calling on him but always found time to taste my wines and talk a little baseball or travel. He always allowed me to bring my own wines and didn't charge corkage, so when we dined there, we'd hand over several bottles to the floor staff to be opened at the appropriate time. When I turned sixty, I had a birthday lunch on Treadwell's patio with a group of Toronto friends. John Brosseau brought a gift bottle of Château de Beaucastel, my favourite wine, but it was a recent vintage that would need a few years in the cellar. It went inside, too, to shelter it from the midday heat of the patio. We informed James of this, but another staff member unwittingly opened the Beaucastel and brought it to the table. John was visibly shaken by this misstep, but James made an amazing recovery. He said calmly that he thought he had an identical bottle in his cellar at home, and he went and got it. He presented it to me, saying, "I know what my girlfriend and I will be drinking tonight," referring to the already opened bottle. Now that's a good sommelier! About three years later, we returned to Treadwell for dinner one night with the now-ready-to-drink Beaucastel and made sure James got a glass.

Marcel Bregstein is the assistant general manager and wine buyer for the Toronto Hunt Club. A finer gentleman you'll never meet, and he purchased

The "Birthday Bunch" at Treadwell's patio (2008).

Calamus wines from me annually for many years, even though he always said his cellar was full. A debonair Costa Rican, Marcel helped me plan our twenty-fifth wedding anniversary and a fiftieth-birthday wine tasting at the Hunt. There is no finer view than sitting on the Hunt Club lawn on the Scarborough Bluffs, where we ended up with a magnum of Veuve Clicquot and cigars on a strikingly beautiful June afternoon. A memorable birthday indeed.

Another long-time customer, continuing until today, is Oakham House at Ryerson University. It took me several tries and changes in managers to get in there, but no one has been more loyal or bought more wine from me over the years. The sales line that finally closed the deal? I had co-founded the first on-campus Ryerson pub in 1971 as a student and it was at Oakham House, so it was fitting that my wine should be sold there. Coincidentally, I met Alice Bannon at that pub in 1971, and we are still together forty-five years later. Some things are meant to be.

Clos Jordanne wins the impromptu Pinot Noir tasting (fall 2015).

The Emerging Ontario Wine Industry Has Arrived

At a recent dinner party, we had an impromptu Burgundy versus Ontario Pinot Noir comparison. Dan Martin, and his travelling wine cellar, provided a Hospices de Beaune and two Gevrey-Chambertins. The sole Ontario entry was a 2010 Clos Jordanne Claystone Terrace, a vineyard that is less than five miles from where we sat. The Burgundies cost in euros what the Claystone did in Canadian dollars. In a unanimous decision, the local product was declared the champ, as has been the case time and time again.

Back in 2009, I teamed up with Thomas Bachelder, then the Clos Jordanne winemaker, to do a formal tasting of Burgundy versus Ontario, both Chardonnay and Pinot Noir. It was done under the auspices of the Niagara chapter of the Ontario Wine Society and held at Niagara College's sensory tasting lab. Forty tasters took part.

Thomas worked in Burgundy and Oregon before taking over at Clos Jordanne and probably knows more about how to make great wine from these two grapes than anyone in Canada. He insisted the tasting be double blind, meaning the tasters wouldn't know what wines were included in the tasting nor their origins. He also insisted that the French wines cost 25 percent more than those from Ontario. Given the cost of Burgundies, this would not be difficult.

The first matchup was between a Clos Vineyard Chardonnay, at $35, and a Meursault, at $57. Thomas told the assembly they should vote as if someone was going to walk in the door and give them a case of the wine they liked best. They preferred the Ontario entry by a margin of three to one. It was not surprising that several years later one of Thomas's Chardonnays beat all comers at an international tasting in Montreal.

The results were similar in the Pinot Noir rounds, Ontario taking two of the three matchups. Ontario had convincingly won the "Judgment at Niagara."

(Sadly, in May 2016, at a barrel tasting at Domaine Queylus, Thomas's latest venture, he announced that Clos Jordanne "is no more." I always felt they had set the benchmark for Ontario Chardonnay and Pinot Noir. It will be interesting to see what happens with Clos Jordanne's single vineyards.)

Two years previously, I presided over another Wine Society blind tasting, Bordeaux versus Ontario meritage blends (ie, blends that contain two or more of the traditional red Bordeaux grapes: Cabernet Sauvignon, Cabernet Franc, Merlot, Petit Verdot, and Malbec). We tasted eight red wines randomly and assigned each a score. The top three wines were local, all from the 2002 vintage – well before Niagara hit its stride in making red wines.

And still you will hear people say that Ontario wines are inferior, there are no good reds, that people won't order them in restaurants, and so on. The reality is that likely no wine region in the world has come so far in such a short time as Niagara.

This progress is thanks to a lot of dedicated people in the local wine industry, and a few just outside of it. One of those was my mentor on the meritage tasting, Larry Paterson, aka Lardy and the Little Fat Wino. Larry was an LCBO employee who railed against the LCBO's lack of support of the local industry at every opportunity. He was also an amateur winemaker who'd obtained Ultimate Master Vintner status in the Amateur Winemakers of Ontario, a level reached by only five other winemakers. He was especially proud of wines made from his beloved Landot grape. Larry promoted Ontario wines with evangelical zeal both inside the LCBO and on his website, where he had reviewed an astonishing number of wines, visiting Niagara wineries at every opportunity. He was an early and true believer that we can make world-class wine here in Ontario.

In 2005, he had organized blind tastings of Bordeaux and Ontario red blends with wine writers, winemakers, and wine educators and judges. The local reds scored higher than the more expensive Bordeaux and took the top five places in a sixteen-bottle tasting. More shockingly, not one of the fifty finely tuned palates could distinguish the fourth- and fifth-growth Bordeaux from the Ontario wines. A year later, I patterned my much smaller tasting after his.

I visited Larry at his Peterborough home in the fall of 2010. He reviewed some Calamus wine that I had brought for dinner and we talked about the Ontario Vinicultural Association that he and Jim Warren had formed to advocate for equal opportunity among Ontario wineries. He was as infuriated as I was to find not a drop of Ontario wine at Ontario Place and gave me a list of some sympathetic MLAs to contact. We finished the evening in his basement, which was festooned with medals and winemaking trophies, for the monthly meeting

Dan Martin, one of Burgundy's best customers.

of his local amateur winemakers' club. I had brought some Horne Brothers offerings that were very well received by the group. Even after the meeting was over, we continued to taste and talk about wine. When I left, he gave me some of his famous chocolate-infused wine. I appreciated the gesture but remain convinced that wine and chocolate should have only a nodding acquaintance.

The next morning, I noticed him labouring heavily, coming up from stirring some lees in the basement. I asked about his health, and he told me he likely needed a lung transplant; a month later, Larry died of pulmonary disease. On Larry's birthday the following June, Michael Pinkus and I organized a tribute to him at Calamus. No one was a more dedicated proponent of the Ontario wine industry than Lardy.

In 2011, the Ontario Wine Awards created the Larry Paterson Award for Innovation in the Vineyard. It's given to the viticulturist who most embodies the passionate values that Larry so tirelessly promoted. The inaugural winner was Deborah Paskus, then winemaker at Closson Chase.

Over the years, I've met some wine writers who have championed the cause of Ontario wine. Tony Aspler, creator of the annual Ontario Wine

Michael Pinkus doing a video from his wine cellar.

Awards; David Lawrason, who has written about Canadian wine since he started *Wine Access* back in the late 1980s; and Konrad Ejbich, who had a long-running monthly wine program on CBC radio, all come to mind.

Someone who was influenced by these writers is the self-proclaimed Grape Guy, Michael Pinkus, who seemingly has made Ontario wine his professional passion while keeping an eye on the international scene. Michael started drinking wine at home as a teen, usually generic German whites, but had his Ontario "awakening" with a bottle of 1999 Château des Charmes Cabernet Merlot with four or five years of age on it. Confirming his belief that Ontario wines could improve with age was a dinner a decade later with the winery's founder, Paul Bosc senior, at which they had the same wine. Pinkus believed Ontario wines were a force to be reckoned with, and he wanted to be part of it. His website and bimonthly newsletter, now up to 267 issues, are a testament to that.

Originally drawn to Niagara by a love of theatre, particularly the Shaw Festival, he started to pay more attention to the emerging wine industry and now makes his living as a writer, social media commentator, magazine columnist, and teacher. He will allow that "making a living" is a tenuous term. As with selling wine "for a living," alternate revenue sources are recommended.

Pinkus believes that the future of Ontario wine will be based on Riesling, Chardonnay, Cabernet Franc, Pinot Noir, and sparkling wine. He warns that wineries will continue to struggle financially, even with grocery-store access on the near horizon. Pinkus feels Ontario consumers are still some years away from fully embracing the local industry.

My brother and I started visiting the Niagara wine region in the late 1980s. There were only a handful of enjoyable wines, made by Inniskillin, Cave Springs, Stoney Ridge, Henry of Pelham, Château des Charmes, Reif, and Hillebrand. The only special wines I remember from that era were Jim Warren's Chardonnays from the Lenko and Eastman vineyards.

Here are some quotes from wine writer Stephen Temkin's **July 1989** report on the Niagara Peninsula:

"Other than Icewine, can we make truly exceptional wine in Ontario?"

"A truly exceptional Chardonnay has yet to be made in Ontario."

"Pinot Noir is showing promise, but I have yet to taste a first-rate example."

"How exciting it would be to travel through the region sampling and buying wines from dozens of small producers, as one can do in Europe."

In rating vinifera wines from the 1988 vintage, Temkin gave no rating over 80 (out of 100), except an 81 for a pair of late-harvest Rieslings.

Obviously, things changed for the better in the ensuing twenty-seven years, making these comments quite humorous today. In his report, Temkin correctly predicts that grape growers must become "wine growers" and be paid accordingly for cropped, high-quality fruit and that the (then) brand-new VQA regulations will help the industry focus on "fine wine." Other steps he suggested, like reforming the LCBO bureaucracy, creating a Niagara green belt, and forming an industry organization, all helped give us the industry we see today.

It's been a great experience to be a small part of the transition from the viticultural wasteland of Temkin's 1989 report to the world-class wines we now all have access to and can be very proud of.

Part of Richard Todd's eclectic wine cellar.

CHAPTER 5

Wine Collecting

I suspect my grandparents never bought wine. I don't remember ever seeing any in either of their homes: one a century farmhouse on Guelph Line, the other a two-storey brick house in Forest, Ontario. My parents' wine collection consisted of a bottle of Mogen David, usually consumed at Christmas, and maybe a bottle of neighbour Walter Kosh's undrinkable swill. Of course, that changed when my brother and I introduced them to wine in the 1970s, but I don't imagine any of them understood the concept of collecting wine or building a wine cellar.

To the best of my reckoning, I figure I've spent a hundred thousand dollars on wine. My wife calls that outrageous, even though she helped drink most of it. I call it a new Mercedes, which I don't have. To many it's a pittance: composer Andrew Lloyd Webber, an infamous hoarder who'd buy hundreds of cases at a time, would spend that in a week; Henry Ford II used his inheritance to buy the good stuff, drinking two bottles of first-growth Bordeaux every night; and the Downton Abbey dining room was never without a red and a white. Judging by Carson's careful husbandry of the wine cellar, it wasn't the cheap stuff.

I wanted a wine cellar for three reasons: to have storage space for wine that needed aging; to have a place to store quantities of wine acquired while travelling, direct from wineries, or in deals too good to pass up; and, most importantly, so that I could go to the cellar and pick just the right wine for the meal or the occasion. If that sounds snobby or finicky, it probably is.

I'd had wine racks before 1986, but when we moved into the house on Dault Road, I found the perfect basement space for a wine cellar. There was a small built-in shelf in the wall for a workspace and shelves to house wine books and the beginnings of thirty years of wine-buying and consumption records. One side of the cellar held Horne Bros wines; the other was for wines I'd bought. Eventually, an iron gate was added to keep out pillaging teenagers while parents were away.

The house, built in 1922, had no air conditioning, and during a hot summer even that corner basement space would warm to dangerous levels for a few weeks. Every time I had a wine that was underwhelming or not up to expectations, I suspected storage conditions. A friend, Fred Collis, asked why I wasn't protecting my investment better. He said that to eliminate the possibility that uneven temperature storage was affecting the wine, I needed to buy a wine storage unit, at least for the expensive stuff. A thousand dollars later, I could rest assured that if a wine wasn't up to snuff, I hadn't ruined it. Twenty years later, I'm still using it, so I guess I've got my money's worth.

When we moved into our St. Catharines townhouse in 2005, a basement storage room cried out "wine cellar." One wall was already covered with shelves that could house my books and binders, as well as my twenty-five-year slide collection. For the other side and the back, I ordered custom redwood wine racks from Strictly Cellars in Mississauga. I designed it to fit the room perfectly and it did, holding about six hundred bottles. Sadly, I never have enough wine to come close to filling it, but wine's for drinking, right?

Bordeaux wine has been called "a minefield of broken dreams," but in 1995, Larry Cook and I began spending hundreds of dollars a year on Bordeaux futures. The idea is that one year after harvest, while the wine is still *en barrique* in France, you make your purchases, putting half the money down and paying the balance on receipt of the bottled wine up to two years later. Futures must be bought in a minimum of three-bottle lots, so we would buy one for each of us and one for a future club tasting. In almost all cases the wine would cost twenty- to twenty-five percent more if you waited for the release. We used the same concept successfully a few years later at Calamus for exceptional Ontario red vintages.

But how to navigate the minefield? We had learned from our collector friend Nico van Duyvenbode that vintages were paramount in Bordeaux and that we should learn which were the undervalued chateaux. This meant researching the Robert Parkers of the world – the handful of critics who have actually tasted the wines, although they would do so *en primeur*, while the wines were still in barrels, maybe a year after the vintage. Eventually Nico himself, who had a house in Bordeaux, started to publish *en primeur* reviews in his newsletter. This all helped us learn the difference between the wines of the Left Bank (Cabernet-based, from the areas south of the Garonne and Gironde rivers) and the Right Bank (Merlot-based from the north of the Dordogne and Gironde) wines, the vintages to buy and those to avoid, and how the good vintages compared to the great ones.

Even after waiting up to three years for the wines to arrive, they usually required several more years of aging, which meant our investment might be tied up for a decade. Very few of them lived up to our expectations, which would be very high after all that waiting, so we gave it up after 2000, or as Larry said, "We'll be drinking it out of straws."

I have seen some awesome wine cellars and collections over the years. My friend René Bertrand built a wonderful walk-in cellar, complete with computerized inventory. He would invite me over to cull some of the older vintages, and some nights more wine went down the drain than down our throats. One of the challenges of having a large cellar is consuming the wine before it's past peak – or worse, undrinkable.

Larry and Heather Malone in Chicago had an equally large walk-in cellar, much of it stocked from the lists of bankrupt restaurants. Larry would casually pull a thirty-year-old Château Latour off the shelf after bypassing several other first growths. Lately, I've been told, they are drinking Dominus after exhausting their supply of Opus One.

Dan Martin has a travelling wine cellar; his substantial collection, mostly acquired in France, is usually in scattered locations or in transit since he moves so much. Whenever he arrives at our place, he needs a case to bring in the night's offering. Twice I have bought a portion of Dan's cellar, when he was moving to Europe, at cut-rate prices. This likely won't happen again, as he has moved back to Canada permanently. The good news is his cellar is now only twenty-five minutes away.

My friend Richard Todd had the most eclectic cellar, in the unfinished basement of his Leslieville house. His place was my home away from home in the years I sold wine in Toronto while living in St. Catharines, and our routine seldom varied. First I would bring in the cases of Calamus he had ordered, then we'd go through every bottle in the cellar to select the night's offerings, usually based on what needed to be drunk. We would start on the main floor, move to the back porch in good weather, and end up in the third-floor "smoking lounge," spinning vinyl and savouring the last drops of one too many bottles.

Bern's Steak House in Tampa has the biggest and most complete cellar I've ever seen, and Barberian's in Toronto is the most impressive I've seen in that city.

Collecting wine has been called a hobby, a fetish, hoarding, a poor investment, or worse. However, I still fantasize about walking into a five-thousand-bottle cellar and selecting the right match for the food, the vintage that needs to be consumed, the second bottle to compare it to – and just to look at all those labels.

The Malones and me in their Chicago cellar.

CHAPTER 6

Diary of a Wine Tourist

Our 1984 trip to Spain started this love affair with wine and began a quest to visit some of the great wine regions of the world – and since grapes are grown almost everywhere on the planet, we have an endless list of destinations to choose from.

Napa / Sonoma

Our first trip was in 1985 with our seven- and four-year-old sons; do that only if you have to. We lived in a trailer that summer and for a week parked it in a campground in the town of Napa. From there we visited some of the bigger names in Napa, like Mondavi, Franciscan and Martini. This was before it was overrun with bus tours and you could buy a five-year-old Inglenook Cabernet Reserve for $15.

Lambert Bridge winery in Sonoma.

Sonoma was rustic by comparison; we stopped at wineries with quirky names like Smothers Brothers and were introduced to new varietals like Gewürztraminer, that lovely but hard-to-pronounce grape. I brought back several bottles to impress my friends in Ontario and dreamed of one day returning to the epicentre of North American wine.

Twenty years later we did, for a five-day stopover on our way to New Zealand and Australia. On our last night in Sonoma, we had dinner at Zazu, a snazzy restaurant outside of Santa Rosa. We started with J Vineyards bubbly, the discovery of the day, then drank our way through the wine-by-the-glass menu, determined to sample all the wineries we had missed over the previous three days. We said goodnight to our travelling companions, back at a bar near our lodgings, over local beer. We packed up our suitcases, including a couple of tasting glasses we'd bought for a picnic lunch the day before, and pulled out our New Zealand maps to put in our carry-on bags along with our passports – and realized mine was missing.

It's a terrible feeling, knowing that no passport means no flight to New Zealand in a few hours – and no prepaid rental car, no expensive hotel room in Auckland that it's too late to cancel, and, since it's Sunday, no open consulate. It was enough to drive a man to drink.

After packing and unpacking our eight pieces of luggage, three times, cursing any manner of responsible people (a short list), and asking my wife for the fourteenth time if she had seen it recently, it was finally found in some now-obvious place that had somehow remained unnoticed in a search that would have made a customs officer proud.

Trip on! It was raining hard in Frisco as the half-full 747 took off for Auckland. We were barely in the air when a lovely Kiwi accent asked me if I'd like some Sauvignon Blanc: "Make mine a double!"

Three days earlier, we had met our friends Anne and Paul in the bar of San Francisco's Adagio Hotel, on Geary Street, and the first of countless nights (and days) of hearty wine drinking began. After a tired Sauvignon Blanc in the bar, we repaired to our room for a real California treat: a Stag's Leap Chardonnay and a terrific 2001 Syrah. Thinking that by 10 pm it must be dinnertime, we trudged up yet another San Fran hill for Thai food with a Washington Gewürtz.

Over the next two days, we went Sideways in Sonoma. There's something magical about leaving San Francisco via the Golden Gate Bridge, a site that welcomed every American serviceman returning from the Pacific in the Second World War. Only the Statue of Liberty is a more recognizable landmark in the United States.

On our first day in wine country, we headed to Glen Ellen for lunch at the Jack London Saloon, which I remembered from our previous trip as one of the most bucolic spots in southern Sonoma. We sat outside with a Benziger Chardonnay – such a treat for two winter-weary Canadians in March. Another old favourite was Cline Cellars, which had the most knowledgeable tasting-room staff I encountered in Sonoma. All in their forties and older, they took us through all the Rhône varietals they are famous for. Nearby Kunde had the biggest barrel cellar I've ever seen, more than six thousand, and Chateau St. Jean is a beautiful French-style château with exquisite wines. At the end of the day it was time for another Benziger Chard in our "tree house" room at the Creekside Inn, deep in the Russian River redwoods. On the way back from dinner (with Zenato Ripasso) at the nearby Applewood Inn, we marvelled at the full moon over the giant redwoods.

We spent another idyllic day driving the rolling hills of Sonoma, visiting old favourites like Rodney Strong and Dry Creek and discovering hidden gems like Lambert Bridge and Everett Ridge, which reminded us of our old-barn start-up winery in the Twenty Valley.

Sonoma Valley is probably my favourite wine destination in the US: it isn't overrun with visitors like Napa is, it has far better wine than the Central Valley or Temecula, and it is just plain comfortable.

Almost every state has wineries now, and there are a handful of good ones in Texas, New Mexico, and Arizona that I've been to, but it's mostly a sea of mediocre or worse wine. The main exception is the Willamette Valley, south of Portland, Oregon, and there's some great Cabernet Sauvignon and Chardonnay coming from Washington State. These are two worthwhile destinations, but I'll take Sonoma anytime.

New Zealand

(*This segment was originally published in the December 2006 issue of* Vines Magazine.)

I wasn't smiling as I got to the front of a long line in Auckland Airport at 5:30 am and was told to get in another line to have our hiking boots fumigated because of a hike in the Redwoods. There is a list as long as your arm of what you can't bring into New Zealand, but we missed that one. An hour later, we reclaimed our now-clean boots, picked up our green Mitsubishi, and ventured into lovely Auckland. New Zealand is a miniature Canada: the North Island is the east and the South Island is the west. Similarly, Auckland is a mini Toronto,

Our first New Zealand winery, Esk Valley.

with its own tower and island (almost), Devonport. When we checked into our hotel suite we discovered the greatest view imaginable. The place, which had been booked by a Toronto agent under tight budget restrictions (the cost of accommodations, especially in cities, on an almost ten-week trip can be prohibitive), had more amenities than our home, including a thirty-foot balcony overlooking the harbour and the bridge. We celebrated with our first bottle of New Zealand Sauvignon Blanc – Kim Crawford, of course, a wine we had fond memories of drinking at a Scottish B&B several years earlier. We cooked dinner in our gourmet kitchen. The sunset from our balcony was outstanding, and so was the Waipara Hills Pinot Noir. I could have stayed right there for a very long time.

We woke to a rainbow over Auckland Harbour and headed south to Lake Taupo, the largest freshwater body in New Zealand or Australia. It's not impressive by Canadian standards, but it's surrounded by geysers, craters, and waterfalls that induced a "Wow, look at that!" around every bend.

After a lovely hot tub at the motel, we set out in search of Thai cuisine and the requisite bottle of Gewürtz to go with it. Almost every Asian restaurant in New Zealand is BYO (bring your own), with a $2 to $4 corkage fee. So you find the eatery, then the bottle shop, as they are so accurately called there, and enjoy a very inexpensive meal out.

By noon the next day, we were enjoying a picnic lunch in the sun with a great bottle of Cab/Merlot, overlooking the picturesque Esk Valley. We visited several wineries that day, including Mission Estate, where I purchased a bottle of Chardonnay "freezer icewine" to take home for comparison. At Mission, we met a couple from Thunder Bay that we would run into at several Hawke's Bay wineries. They took their wine tasting seriously: for two months, they had been going to six wineries a day Down Under and had made notes on every wine they tasted. A couple of days later, we were in CJ Pask winery near Hastings telling a young couple from Michigan about these dedicated oenophiles, and in they walked, right on cue, notebooks in hand.

We stayed in a suburb of Napier while touring Hawke's Bay. We called it Pleasantville: everything was perfectly manicured, squeaky clean, and everyone pleasant and smiling. Adding to the surreal feel was the fact that Napier had been destroyed by an earthquake in the early 1930s and had been entirely rebuilt in the Art Deco style of the day. The humorous and knowledgeable "pour girls" in wineries like Kim Crawford, Esk River, and Mission Estate make this area one of the best cellar-door (as they call tasting rooms Down Under) experiences you will ever find.

Martinborough is one of New Zealand's lesser known and smaller wine areas but should not be missed. It's not far out of the way when driving from Auckland to Wellington, and if you don't mind the occasional sheep herd blocking the country roads you travel, you'll be rewarded with a memorable wine experience. The town itself has a population of no more that two thousand, but it has a wine centre where you can taste and purchase all the region's wines and have a café lunch. While visiting Palliser (one of my favourite Pinot Noir producers), a young woman named Leah convinced us to dine at the Est Wine Bar, where she also worked. After checking into the Swan B & B, where we had a huge windowed room surrounded by lawns and willows, we walked into town and were wowed by the food, service, and wine selection at Est. I started with my first New Zealand beer (took a while to work that in) and then moved to glasses from producers with challenging Maori names like Te Kairanga and Ata Rangi. On the starry walk home, we were happy not to be driving, particularly on the left-hand side.

Wellington is a more hip, happening city than Auckland with a stunning location on the Tasman Sea. Much of the city is built into hillsides; the cable car ride from the town centre to the top of the Botanic Garden is a must. During our visit, an Italian wine-and-food festival was going on at the harbour and there were plenty of lively pubs and bars. We chose another BYO restaurant on a street full of them, near our hotel, buying a $12 Timara Cab/Merlot and a Kim Crawford Chardonnay on the way. One must be prepared for any food eventuality.

Not only do you travel east to west on the three-hour sail to the South Island, but Wellington in the North is further south than Picton, the South Island terminus – got that? If that's not confusing enough, at our first stop, Cloudy Bay Estates, there was no water to be seen. But no matter: we were now in Marlborough, the holy grail of New Zealand wines.

Cloudy Bay, effectively, launched the Kiwi wine revolution, taking London by storm with their Sauvignon Blanc in the mid-1990s. I remember seeing a sign in front of a Kiwi wine bar near Leicester Square in 1995 that warned "No Cloudy Bay today." Today the winery is owned by an international conglomerate and produces overpriced wine, including a Sauvignon Blanc aged in ten-year-old oak barrels. The only red they make is an underwhelming Pinot Noir.

To get the real thing in Pinot, we needed only to travel a few kilometres down the road to Herzog, the best red wine producer in New Zealand. Hans Herzog moved from Switzerland in the late 1990s with a plan to make great European-style vinifera wine in Marlborough. The red wines we tasted that day were stunning and served in big Riedel glasses to give the full effect. These wines come into Vintages occasionally; they are expensive but worth it, especially the Pinot Noir. Hans, despite fleeing the Old World for the New, is somewhat of a traditionalist. The screwcap revolution is over in New Zealand: of the thirty-six wineries we visited, every current vintage was in Stelvin closures – except Herzog. I can't imagine Hans changing any time soon.

As so often happens in the world of wine, just when you think you've reached the mountaintop, there's another one waiting. In this case, it was a short trip down the road. At Nautilus, the Reserve Pinot Noir was simply the best New World Pinot I've ever tasted. The depth of fruit and beguiling aroma would have given Miles from *Sideways* an orgasm. Only four barrels of this velvet seductress were made; we'll never see it here in Ontario. I spent the rest of the trip regretting that I didn't pull the trigger on the $47 price tag. We later tasted $60 to $70 offerings that could only stand in its shadow; I was at the mountaintop but didn't know it.

The next day we finally saw the real Cloudy Bay. After hiking to the top of the Wither Hills, looking out over the Wairau Valley and the town of Blenheim, it looked mysterious and, well, cloudy in the distance. Wither Hills is also a winery, of course, in a brand new building and with new corporate owners. It was there we had the best Chardonnay of the trip, and for only $25.

Nelson is the gateway to Abel Tasman National Park, where we hiked the most spectacular trail I've ever been on, much of it overlooking the Tasman Sea. After twelve kilometres, we toasted our success, on a beach that could

Lunch at Waitiri Creek in Central Otaga.

have been in the Caribbean, with a fetching rosé from Gladstone Vineyard, run by a Scottish woman on the North Island. It was definitely not lolly water, the name rosé detractors give it Down Under.

We then called a water taxi to take us back. The tide was out, so a tractor with trailer came down to the water, loaded up the boat with sixteen people and dropped us at our car, all for $20. Back in our hostel on the main street of Nelson, we cooked a salmon in butter and herbs and consumed it with the splendid Wither Hills Chardonnay, a match made in heaven.

There are some impressive wines to be tasted in the Nelson area, including a stunning off-dry Riesling at Waimea Estates. The best cellar-door experience in New Zealand may be at Te Mania Estates, whose Grape Escape complex includes a candle and art shop, a café for tour groups, and a grape grower behind the tasting bar serving wines from three different wineries. We were there for almost two hours; the only downside was the four-hour drive over the mountains to the scenic west coast that was up next.

There was not a gas station to be seen on the whole trip, and the last half hour was spent in a desperate search for petrol. We came to a fork in the road. Should we go the direction we were headed or the opposite way, which offered a better chance to shut off the annoying "fuel empty" light that seemed to have been on for hours? As the sun set over the Tasman Sea in spectacular fashion, we coasted into a gas station, then headed for the Greymouth Hotel and a few Monteith's ales to calm our shattered nerves.

The trip down the west coast of New Zealand's South Island is one of the world's most scenic. There are glaciers only slightly above sea level, picture-perfect lakes like Matheson, waterfalls, and snow-capped peaks. Even the rain there (the first we'd had) didn't dampen our spirits. We leaned heavily on our travelling wine cellar accumulated in Marlborough and Nelson to get us through to Queenstown and the nearby Central Otaga wine district.

The trip from the west coast to Queenstown through the Southern Alps, always with a lake in view, is like watching *Lord of the Rings* without the actors. Queenstown itself is a lively town of 7,500 on a long lake called Wakatipu. It's the home of all sports extreme, with paragliders constantly dropping out of the sky.

Saturday night started with a Goldwater Cabernet Merlot at a Mexican BYO joint called Sombreros. After dinner we decided to avail ourselves of some local nightlife. There is a plethora of bars and clubs in Queenstown and plenty of under-thirties to populate them. It's quite a scene, and the almost carless streets are jammed with partiers. We found an Irish pub called Pog Mahones with a young Canadian entertainer and settled into our Bushmills and Kilkenny. He covered it all, from Irish drinking songs to Rod Stewart, and had a large table of well-refreshed young lasses dancing and singing along all night.

It was with less than clear heads we started our tour of Otaga the next day. Heading east toward Cromwell, we had to decide which of the thirty-six wineries to visit and got remarkably lucky. A huge tour bus pulled into Gibbston Valley winery ahead of us, so we kept going down the road to Peregrine, just moved into a new facility and making great Pinot. After a lengthy chat with a couple from Albany, New York, whose daughter was going to "uni" in Brisbane, we picked out (they had four to choose from) our $35 Pinot for dinner and went to Waitiri Creek for lunch. The tasting room and restaurant are in an old church. We ate on the lawn in a beautiful setting, enjoying chicken and venison with large glasses of Chardonnay and Pinot, while we marvelled at the scenery around us. (Five years later, we would use Waitiri for an emergency bathroom stop, knowing that the facilities were outside.)

The road into the Chard Farm winery (it's actually the family name) is not for the faint hearted. It's narrow, has no guardrail, and there's a straight drop of hundreds of feet. I couldn't look down until we stopped on a turn where there was actually room for two cars to pass. Looking across the chasm, we could see a crowd watching people bungee jumping off a bridge. We later learned that this is where it originated – across from a winery … I wonder? Chard Farm was worth the harrowing journey: it had fabulous wines (especially the Pinots), an interesting history, and, of course, a stunning view.

We now had time for only one more New Zealand winery: Amisfield, just outside of Queenstown, specialized in bubbly and stickies, the endearing name Kiwis (and Aussies) give to dessert wines. As we sipped through their well-crafted offerings, we reflected on the past two weeks, the thirty-plus wineries, and the many experiences we'd enjoyed. We realized that one day we would have to come back and visit the half of New Zealand we didn't get to.

Australia

While spending three days in the fabulous city of Sydney, we met up with a former co-worker of Alice's and her husband on a stunningly beautiful late afternoon in Darling Harbour. He had the enviable position of fine wine specialist for Gallo wines, and they had just returned from Hunter Valley, our first wine destination. They gave us many tips, and our excitement increased ac-

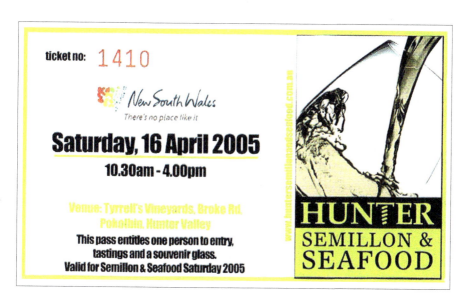

Tasting with Terry at Ilnam Estate.

cordingly as we sipped our Verdelho, a fruity, lightly spiced white grown almost exclusively in Portugal, Spain, and Australia that he had introduced us to.

Our first Hunter stop, after checking in to the Cessnock Vintage Motor Inn, was at Mount Pleasant, a winery represented in North America by Gallo. After dropping the "right name," we were treated royally by a twenty-year-old pour guy. He really knew his stuff and educated us on Semillon, the signature white grape of Hunter Valley. We left with our first free bottle, a 2000 Semillon. (Full disclosure here: I usually mentioned Horne Brothers Fine Wines and the vineyards we'd leased to grow grapes at some point in our tasting-room conversations, and the result was often remarkable, including free bottles. The magic phrase was "growers from Canada.")

Our next stop was Lindeman's, makers of the globally popular Bin 65 Chardonnay. The staff there called it their Big Mac, as in billions sold. Much like Foster's beer, it's mostly for export. They treated us to a bevy of old vintages, and we came away with a ten-year-old Semillon, which we drank that evening, no further cellaring required.

The next day we met Damien Evans, who managed the Small Winemakers Centre, a concept we could really use in Ontario: a collective cellar door for six small wineries. Damien was perhaps the most entertaining and knowledgeable "wine guy" I have ever met. It was morning and we had him to ourselves for an hour and a half. We enjoyed great wine conversation, plenty of under-the-counter pours, and two good tips: have dinner at the Australia Hotel in Cessnock, it's where the locals go; and spend the rest of the day at the Semillon and Seafood Festival at Tyrrell's Wines, about fifteen minutes away.

A $15 entry fee got us a tasting glass and wine from thirty-five wineries, but only Semillon, in all its forms, from dry to sticky. There were lots of old vintages, as Semillon ages very well, and a vast array of delicious salmon, scallops, and more to try them with. Add some great live music from an all-girl band called Bella and it was an afternoon of pure pleasure.

The harvest in Hunter ends in early April, and temperatures often reach 40 Celsius, so we moved to a higher-altitude area to get the structure I like in reds. This also meant having our first taste of Oz bubbly at a winery called Petersons that specializes in sparkling wine. The last stop was at Briar Ridge, and after a long conversation about microclimates, netting, and sugar levels, the owner gave us a private tasting. At the end he produced his pride and joy, a cold-soaked Cabernet Sauvignon, with good acidity and structure and lower alcohol – my favourite red from this very hot region.

We reluctantly left Hunter, moving up the coast, staying in small coastal towns like Hawks Nest and Nambucca Heads. As we headed to Coffs Harbour to watch the surfers, we found one lonely winery named Cassegrain. It turned out to have better wines than most in the Hunter and a sublimely beautiful and engaging pour girl. Aussie Shiraz is not my favourite, but I walked out of there with a magnum, which came in handy at a BYO Malaysian restaurant in Brisbane a couple of weeks later with a group of new friends and one from thirty years previous, Terry Thomas.

We hadn't seen Terry since travelling in Europe in the mid '70s. He had invited us to stay with him at his off-the-grid house, halfway up a mountain near the village of Nimbin, the marijuana capital of Australia.

To my amazement, Terry had a wine cellar, which he said needed "sorting out," which, it turned out, meant drinking up all the old vintages. Some were resigned to Alice's reduction sauce, but there were many long-forgotten treasures, especially from Château Tanunda in Barossa Valley. We drank like kings every night and toured the surrounding area every day. The only winery in the area was Ilnam Estate, near the town of Tweed, so inevitably we ended up there one day. The location was spectacular, with a far-away ocean view, terraced vineyards, and a loggia-style patio for tasting. I said the magic words to owner Mark Quinn, a dead ringer for a young Mel Gibson, and he produced barrel samples of Petit Verdot and Shiraz before the official tasting. Our wine conversation continued over a lunch of cheese, bread, olive oil, and a cold bottle of Chardonnay, as we gazed out over the magnificent view.

Heather Roland was waiting for us at the Adelaide Airport; we had not seen her in twenty years. As it turned out, she had a wine cabinet that also needed sort-

With the winemaker at Château Yaldara.

ing out, and we cut a wide swath through her collection. They were all exceedingly drinkable, so much that our planned trip to McLaren Vale the next day got off to a slow start, but we soldiered on and by 1 pm were tasting the fruit of the vine again with a Grenache grower who later directed us to our next stop. The owners of Foggo had supplied grapes for Penfolds Grange Hermitage, Australia's most celebrated wine, for many years before deciding to start bottling their own products. They were away for a couple of days and had left Bob, a wine tour operator, in charge. He regaled us with stories and pulled out all the good stuff to impress the Canadian growers. The wines were absolutely stunning, and we would never have heard of the place if not for the conversation with the Grenache grower.

My favourite Australian winery is d'Arenberg, where we dined overlooking the vineyards. They are known for their Rhône varietals, such as Viognier, Roussanne, Grenache, and Mourvèdre, and do a masterful job of blending. Their vineyards are cropped to less than 1.5 tons per acre to produce intense fruit. I think d'Arenberg is one of the world's great wineries and buy their whites, especially, whenever I can.

We also spent a day in nearby Coonawarra, a region known for its Cabernet Sauvignon. We avoided the mammoth Wynns and spent quality time at Parker, which makes Cab Sauv and Merlot only, and Bowen Estate, which specializes in Chardonnay and Shiraz. We were the only people in these wineries, each of which makes only five thousand cases each year; these small producers tend to be where the best wine and the superlative tasting experiences are to be found.

The "promised land" of Australian wine is the Barossa Valley, about forty-five kilometres northeast of Adelaide. We arrived in Tanunda, the central town, late on a Wednesday, sans reservation. We had to settle for an old hotel on the main street that featured a sixty-foot balcony where we enjoyed the best pizza of the trip and a bottle of exquisite d'Arenberg Viognier. We spent the whole night listening to heavy trucks rumble by and the next morning headed directly to the local information centre in search of better accommodation. What we found was a little bit of heaven, called Woodbridge: our own two-bedroom cottage on a sheep farm with a fifty-acre vineyard, a tennis court, and full provisions for breakfast. We booked for three nights. The owners, Bill and Penny Holmes, were wonderful hosts. Bill was a retired dentist who had planted vines in 1998, and Penny had grown up on a sheep farm.

They recommended some smaller wineries to visit, and we had a huge hit on the first one, Château Yaldara. After the usual tasting and conversation, the pourer got the general manager, Lisa Miranda, who promptly opened a $120 older Shiraz for us to try and sent for the winemaker, Thomas Jung. Nothing would do but to taste a range of his barrel samples. Some other customers and staff joined in, and a party broke out in the tasting room. It was one of those joyous spontaneous moments in the world of wine.

Lisa sent us on to her father's winery, where we bought three bottles, including a real surprise: he was the Aussie agent for Lanson Champagne. A bottle of Black Label was later opened to celebrate our fiftieth day on the road at Apollo Bay, on the Great Ocean Road. (Second disclosure: I had been commissioned by *Vines* magazine to do a story on New Zealand and always had a copy on me. I occasionally played this card in Australia and had done so at Yaldara.)

I have always been amazed at the difference that enthusiasm and passion make in the enjoyment of the wine in a tasting-room setting. Later that day, we tasted at Two Hands with a joyless, morose Argentine who never smiled once. Although the wines were correct and well made, we left without purchasing.

Someone with a ton of passion and knowledge was Jane Ferrari, the winemaker and chief communicator at Yalumba. She was summoned to the tasting room, resplendent in a sweatshirt, and gave us horizontal tastings of their various Viogniers, Rieslings, and Grenaches. We quickly bonded over the fact that she had recently done a wine sampling at the Toronto Hunt Club, the site of our twenty-fifth wedding anniversary and my fiftieth birthday lunch and tasting.

After a long day of imbibing, we arrived back at our cottage to find a note on the door from Bill Holmes, complete with hand-drawn map, inviting us to the annual tasting and barbecue of the Gomersal growers' association. Bill promised "an excellent array of Australian wines," so of course we went.

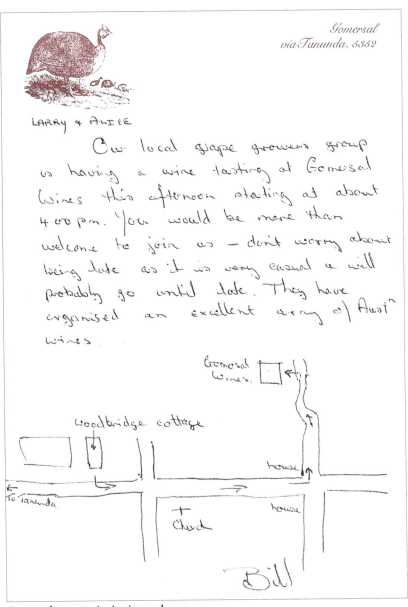

Gomersal growers invitation and map.

We arrived for the fortified portion of the tasting, led by Dean, who had been a winemaker for Penfolds and others for more than 30 years. His wit and experience made for a memorable evening. We were introduced by Will Holmes, who looked after the family vineyard, as "growers from Canada." The rest of the night was spent fielding questions on Icewine and sampling all the growers' favourite wines. Many of them still couldn't believe we can grow grapes in Canada.

Our credentials now established, we were invited to a sit-down vertical tasting of Charles Melton's fabled Nine Popes, the Oz version of Châteauneuf-du-Pape. Next, VIP treatment at Peter Lehmann, including a free bottle of Clancy's Red, a trip through old vintages of E&E Black Pepper Shiraz at Barossa Valley Estate, and tastings with the owners at Rockford Wines and Whistler.

Our last stop in Barossa was at the giant Wolf Blass facility, just ahead of a bus tour, fortunately. Wolf Blass put the region on the international wine map, and it was there that I became convinced that the future of closures would be screwcaps: they had begun putting their Platinum line of wines in Stelvin. We bought the Chardonnay to have on our last day of the trip after nine and a half weeks in Sonoma, New Zealand, and Australia.

As we reluctantly said farewell to our wine paradise, the Holmes gave us a bottle of Shiraz from their vineyard, and we had a look at some newborn lambs. This had been the pinnacle of our Aussie experience. Barossa is truly one of the world's great wine regions, the people as well as the wine.

Germany

The trip down the Rhine, especially from Cologne to Mainz, is spectacular: castles, cathedrals, terraced vineyards, and quaint wine villages at every turn. Just south of Rüdesheim, the river turns west to east for thirty kilometres; this area is called the Rheingau, the undisputed home of Germany's most classic Riesling, due in part to the unique conditions and terroir. Armed with Stuart Pigott's book *Life Beyond Liebfraumilch*, we headed for the village of Walluf, right in the middle of the Rheingau. There, according to Pigott, could be found the best Riesling producer in the area, Hans-Josef Becker.

It was a weekday afternoon, August 28, 1991, and there was no one to be found as we roamed the winery property, even going in and out of the house. Just as we were about to give up and move on to the next village, a wiry, blond-haired figure appeared, coming out of the vineyard. He appeared to be mid-forties and sported a majestic walrus moustache. He greeted us in perfect English, explaining that he was "not open to visitors currently." I responded by saying, "Stuart Pigott says you are the best Riesling producer in the Rheingau, and we have come all the way from Canada to find out."

That bit of flattery seemed to work. He smiled for the first time and said, "Ah yes, Mr. Pigott," introduced himself, and said, "Why don't you come

Chatting with Hans-Josef Becker in Der Weingarten.

with me?" The next four to five hours was one of my favourite wine experiences ever.

We stood in his vineyard and talked for a few minutes about the vines his grandfather had planted, and after deeming me sufficiently serious and knowledgeable (I suppose), we got the grand tour of the winery, picking out wines to be purchased as we went. At one point, Becker was standing precariously at the top of a ladder, in the old barn, rummaging through cases in search of a 1971 Wallufer Walkenberg Auslese, the first vintage he had made on his own. This wine did make it home and was part of a Noble Rotters tasting; it may have been the finest Riesling I've ever tasted. He then suggested we try his favourite wine, amazingly not a Riesling, but a Spatburgunder, aka Pinot Noir. Becker was in love with the grape and had travelled to Burgundy several times to learn techniques such as egg-white fining.

At this point, I thought we might have worn out our welcome, so we paid for our case of wines and were about to say goodbye. Little did I know, things were just getting started. Hans-Josef insisted we cross the road to where his sister, Maria, operated Becker's Wine Garden on the banks of the Rhine. It was shortly after five, and the place was already buzzing with after-work imbibers. Hans-Josef found us a quiet table adjacent to the bar, introduced us to Maria, and the wines and conversation flowed for the next couple of hours. All thoughts of driving to Heidelberg that night, as planned, were abandoned, and we bunked in at the nearby Hotel Ruppert for the night. We never got a bill from Der Weingarten, and I have never forgotten the Beckers. I recently was shown a Facebook picture of him closing the wine garden for the season, still sporting the moustache, now grey but just as majestic.

We continued drinking our way down the Rhine, with an especially interesting private tasting at Guntrum, a producer familiar to me from the LCBO. In fact, they proudly showed us a skid of cases about to be shipped to the Queen's Quay distribution centre in Toronto. At Guntrum, we were able to taste all the ripeness-at-harvest levels (unlike terroir-based hierarchies in other Old World wine regions, German wines are classified based on how ripe producers can get their grapes before picking), from Kabinett through to Trockenbeerenauslese (TBA), as well as other varietals such as Silvaner, Scheurebe, Müller-Thurgau, Gewürztraminer, and Bacchus – a very intense German wine experience that sent us on our way to meet an old friend in Strasbourg with another case of wine in the trunk of our rental car.

Alsace

I grew up with Steve Coomber on Oakridge Drive in Scarborough. Now living in Fribourg, Switzerland, he had agreed to meet us in Strasbourg and travel the Alsatian wine route to Colmar. It's only eighty kilometres along the eastern side of the Vosges mountains, but in between lay some of the world's great vineyards and dozens of wine villages with fabled names like Riquewihr (home of Dopff & Irion and Hugel) and Ribeauvillé (Trimbach), all displaying many signs shouting out *"Degustation."* It was a daunting task to try to cover this in one day, especially in light of the damage done catching up over way too many Kronenbourg beers at a sidewalk café beside the Strasbourg cathedral. At breakfast the next morning, we desperately wanted good strong coffee but instead were served large bowls of brownish warm water.

Nonetheless, we were at our first *degustation* in Obernai by 10:15 am. I have always loved Alsatian wines; no region can equal the breadth of the region's white wine styles, from Riesling through the seven other varieties grown there, plus Pinot Noir. What a treat: sampling the best Pinot Gris, Pinot Blanc, Muscat, and Gewürztraminer the world has to offer in each beguiling village, not to mention the occasional palate cleanse with Crémant d'Alsace, the regional sparkler. By the time we reached Colmar and found Brasserie Heydel, the recommended dining spot, it was the traditional house wine, Edelzwicker, for us. Sometimes the simplest wine will suffice.

Champagne

It has been scientifically proven that there are forty-nine million bubbles in a bottle of Champagne. (Look it up!) Like Oscar Wilde, I regret not drinking enough of it. We did not make that mistake when visiting Épernay, La Capitale du Champagne. Épernay is the home of several stately Champagne houses, including Taittinger, Perrier-Jouët, Pol Roger (Churchill's favourite), and, most famously, Moët & Chandon. It is said that every second somewhere in the world, a bottle of Moët pops its cork. The namesake of its iconic brand, a sixteenth-century Benedictine monk named Dom Perignon who was cellar master at his abbey, apparently only tasted before breakfast, to ensure a perfectly clear palate. We did the best we could by arriving at 9:30 am at the two-hundred-year-old château fittingly located on the Avenue de Champagne.

As you enter the vast cellars that run twenty-five kilometres and hold fifty million bottles, you see a large painting of Napoleon drinking a glass of Champagne on the very spot you are standing. He was one of Moët's best customers, along with most of Europe's royal courts. Apparently Moët's grandson and Napoleon were military cadets together, and the emperor toasted every military victory with Moët champagne, introducing it to the world outside France.

On the tour, you learn about the complex *méthode champenoise*, which involves a secondary fermentation that produces the bubbles; "riddling," the inverting and daily turning of the bottles; and "disgorging," the freezing of the liquid in the bottle neck to expel the dead yeast cells. Finally, a mixture of wine and sugar, the dosage, is added to determine the wine's sweetness, and a cork-and-wire muzzle completes the process. This process takes three to fours years, and by French law, only Chardonnay, Pinot Noir, and Pinot Meunier grapes can be used in Champagne's production. The tour ended with a long-awaited tasting of several vintages and types of Moët products – but no "Dom" for us tourists.

Although Champagne usually has less than 13 percent alcohol, the theory that it goes "straight to your head" because the bubbles carry the alcohol into your bloodstream quicker, proved to be correct. I'm not sure what we did for the rest of the afternoon, but I know that at dinner, in a cozy restaurant called Le Théâtr' Gourmand, I ordered my long-time favourite, Lanson Black Label. Victor Lanson was reputed to have drunk seventy thousand bottles of Champagne in his lifetime and lived to be eighty-seven – no regrets there.

Switzerland

Swiss wines are very correct and generally expensive – that is to say, very Swiss. Most of the vineyards are in western Switzerland, especially along the Lake Geneva shoreline between Lausanne and Montreux. In the heart of that wine-growing region is the town of Vevey.

Vevey has long been home to the rich and famous, from Charlie Chaplin to Shania Twain, and is the heart of the Swiss Riviera, complete with palm trees and casinos. (It is also the international headquarters of Nestlé.) Our friend Anne picked us up at the station and drove a ways up the mountain to her home in Corseaux to drop off our bags because we had a 6 pm date for a wine tasting at Domaine Bovy. We were right in the middle of Lavaux, the best white wine region *en Suisse*, terraced vineyards all around us.

Anne's boyfriend, Jean-Vincent, was part of the family-owned winery and had arranged for us to meet with Eric Bovy. We tasted several whites – Chasselas, Viognier, and Chardonnay – got a tour and found much in common between Calamus and Bovy, despite their larger size (fifteen thousand cases) and century headstart. We bought four wines and were gifted two more. I left them a Vidal Icewine, and we swapped winery baseball caps. I wondered why we had tasted no reds. When we returned to Anne's, I discovered the reason: Jean-Vincent had three of them lined up (Bordeaux and Gamay/Pinot blends) alongside a delicious lamb dinner. While we were waiting for dinner, we treated ourselves to a 2005 Fixin I had brought from Burgundy.

Legendary perch and rosé lunch on Lake Neuchâtel.

We met the next day with heavy heads, and after a serious hike in the Alps we made dinner plans. The restaurant we chose, in a nearby village, had a complete Chaplin theme. Turned out it was the village he lived in until his death in 1977, and his son was still a customer. Five-hundred-millilitre bottles are quite popular in Switzerland and help solve the dilemma of red or white; also, we were still chastened from the previous night's excess.

On our last night in the area, we drove into Vevey for Foire aux Vins, which featured thirty-plus wine and food booths, sort of a mini gourmet-wine-and-food show. I tried only Pinot Noirs, the red grape that does the best in this area, and some were more than respectable. We finished the night with steak tartare, lamb and rice, and two more bottles of Bovy red back at the villa. I now had a new appreciation for Swiss wines.

However, my most enduring Swiss memory is still a September 1991 lunch on a boat on Lake Neuchâtel enjoying a delightful perch meal with two bottles of Oeil de Perdrix (the local rosé) and our friends the Boyers – European living at its finest.

Burgundy

I've heard good Burgundy described as "like true love: elusive but worth the search"; I've been disappointed many times. Author Frank Harris described it as "a woman in her thirties, mature bodied, richer, more generous, with a finer perfume; but it is very intoxicating and should be used with self-restraint."

I first visited Burgundy in 1991, staying in Beaune at the Hôtel de la Cloche, which serves the finest croissant I've ever had. Beaune is right in the middle of the fabled Côte d'Or and the best spot from which to explore the region. We headed north, for Nuits-Saint-Georges first, driving by all the magical village and vineyard names: Clos de Vougeot, Chambolle-Musigny, Romanée-Conti, and finally Aloxe-Corton, my personal holy grail. My first taste of real red Burgundy, only a few years before, was a 1971 Aloxe-Corton that my friend John Brosseau had brought from Century Liquor in Rochester, New York. It cost the princely sum of $25 and it was fabulous; I was hooked on a habit that I now, since retiring, cannot afford.

We purchased and tasted at Corton and other wineries, but we had the ultimate sampling experience at the Marché aux Vins in Beaune: a huge underground cave filled with candlelit barrels, each topped with a selection of wines, starting with Chardonnays, then Beaujolais, and finally *cru* reds: the wines made from grapes grown in named vineyards designated either premier or grand cru ("growth"). It took two hours to navigate our way through it,

10 am tasting at Domaine Jessiaume.

drinking out of the traditional shallow silver *tastevin* cups that French sommeliers have used for years. Never had I tasted so much great wine at one time – and all before noon! We emerged bleary-eyed into the sunlight of a beautiful September day and headed off for a long Burgundian lunch.

It would be exactly twenty years before we returned to Burgundy, a trip organized by fellow wine enthusiast Dan Martin. Dan contacted me from his home in Switzerland, saying he had made reservations at a hotel in Beaune and hoped we would approve. It was Hôtel de la Cloche. I replied, "It's the only place we stay in Beaune." I was already looking forward to the croissants.

We drove out of Neuchatel, Switzerland, on a rainy Friday afternoon with Dan and arrived in Beaune around 6 pm. We had arranged to meet our friends Bill and Colleen Boyer in the hotel bar, where our first wine, a 2006 Beaune white, had to be sent back, oxidized and undrinkable – not a good start. We fared much better with an '09 Pernand-Vergelesses and then walked the cobblestone streets across town to Beaune Francette for a late dinner. The food was fabulous; I had coq au vin and coquilles St.-Jacques, both divine. We had two reds, an '07 Aloxe-Corton from Maillard and an '05 Chassagne-Montrachet. The '05 turned out to be the benchmark we sought all weekend but couldn't find again, definitely the best value wine, and the vintage was drinking perfectly.

Saturday at 10 am found us at Domaine Jessiaume in Santenay, about twenty minutes southwest of Beaune. Although the winery had been bought re-

A long lunch at La Table de Pierre Bourée.

cently by a Scottish lord, it was still a fifth-generation family-run operation. We had a full tour of the ancient cellars, where we saw wines from the early 1900s. Each vintage is recorked every 25 years or disposed of. This winery is so successful that there were no whites available – they'd all been sold – but we did taste a 2010 tank sample that had already been oak aged. Dan would return to buy several cases of this wine.

We had a private tasting with our host, a family member probably mid-twenties, in a beautiful 18th-century drawing room. Of six wines, he did not spit one, and it was 11 am.

The Pinots were all 2009s, ranging from 23 euros for premier cru to 45 euros for a grand cru. We bought plenty, and these wines came home, as they needed time.

Next we drove to Gevrey-Chambertin at the other end of the Côte d'Or for lunch at the unique La Table de Pierre Bourée. It was owned by a winery, and you could have a five-, seven-, or nine-glass degustation with a meal of several courses. We went for the seven-glass option, which took us through two whites and five reds, progressing from simple Bourgogne to village-level, to premier cru and grand cru. After this two-and-a-half-hour lunch, we could buy any of the wines we had enjoyed with the meal. I went for an '09 Marsannay white and a 2000 Charmes-Chambertin, which did not make it home.

We barely made our 3:30 appointment in Meursault back in the south. Boyer-Martenot is a white specialist; in fact, the three reds we tasted were awful. There is bad wine in Burgundy, but I did gain an appreciation for Aligoté, a grape that I have trashed repeatedly over the years. Yes it's simple, but at 8 euros, it's better value than anything you can buy in Switzerland. The tasting went on forever: I'm certain I've bought a car in less time than it took to check out the '09 Meursault, a Puligny-Montrachet, and the Aligoté (good wines but not stunning). The French take their time when it comes to tasting wine.

Back at the hotel, it was Kir time for me, a fondly remembered local tradition that mixes Cassis and white wine. Then off to find a restaurant on Saturday night without reservations – that's called living dangerously in France.

After a couple of rebuffs, we found Cheval Blanc, near Hotel Dieu, and had a lovely meal, complete with beef bourguignon for me. We also had a French waiter out of central casting; first he ignored us for a long time, and then he wanted everything to happen quickly. He wouldn't let us order wine first, in case it wasn't right for the meal, he said. By the time he let us order the wine I had forgotten our picks, and under pressure from him I ordered an '08 white from Remoissenet and, I thought, an '08 Gevrey-Chambertin. He brought an '07, a poor vintage that I would never have knowingly ordered, which he quickly opened and poured for everyone. No presentation of the bottle or offer to taste. After we all tried it and were underwhelmed, I noticed, after putting my glasses on, the vintage. We called the waiter over and sent it back! We heard him say, at least three times, now in perfect English to the whole room, that he would be paying for the wine and not to worry. What we did worry about was what he might have done to the desserts! The meal and wine were 223 euros (for five) and a very large tip.

Still in search of the elusive '05s, we stopped at the Brasserie Le Belena, where we had dined twenty years ago, and picked an '05 Chambolle-Musigny off the list, but it still didn't match up to the Chassagne-Montrachet from Friday night that was half the price.

Sunday morning, Dan and I went shopping specifically for '05 Pinots. Most wineries are closed on Sundays, but the wine shops in Beaune are open, and it was a glorious fall day after two days of rain. I found a Faiveley Nuits-Saint-Georges and a Fixin, but the '05s were few and far between. I couldn't bring myself to buy either of the grand crus that were 80 euros and up without tasting them.

We checked out of La Cloche and headed south to Rully and a restaurant Dan knew well from previous visits, Le Vendangerot. Lunch started with a round of Crémant de Bourgogne, then a *demi bouteille* of Saint-Véran white for those having the scallops and a Rully premier cru for the meat eaters. I completed my French food triumvirate with *magret de canard*. All the local wines were the same price: 29 euros for the village selections and 30 euros for the premier crus. Very odd pricing, but as it turns out it was *vin ordinaire* after what we had been tasting all weekend. The food, however, was delightful.

After visiting the war memorial in this quaint village, we once again headed north to Beaune to visit Bouchard Père & Fils, one of the large wineries that's supposed to be open Sundays; it wasn't, so we walked around the corner to Patriarche Père et Fils (*depuis* 1780). We declined the 10 euro tour of their cellars that extend two kilometres under the streets of Beaune followed by a tasting, but we did the gift shop extensively, and I managed to pick up one more '05 and a Crémant. Sunday-night dinner back in Neuchâtel was salted peanuts and water.

Tuscany

After one visit, you spend the rest of your life wondering why you haven't moved to Tuscany, or at least gone back several times. Similar to Provence with its hilltop villages, stunning scenery, and Roman history, it offers decidedly better wines. The reds are mostly from the Sangiovese grape and clones such as Brunello, and in recent years, Cabernet Sauvignon has added complexity to the so-called super-Tuscans.

Our Chicago friends the Malones were veteran visitors to the area and suggested a wonderful villa just north of Siena that was also a working winery. A lovely bottle of their white awaited us in our room on arrival. From there, we could head out each day to nearby legendary wine villages, including Montalcino, Montepulciano, and San Gimignano, all stunningly beautiful with beguiling wines. On days we wanted to stay closer to home, we had dozens of nearby Chianti Classico wineries to visit.

We would often arrive home in late afternoon, sit in our *loggia*, and drink one of our prized purchases from the day with bread, olive oil, and cheese. Then it was a home-cooked meal or a short trip to a local *ristorante* before watching the fireflies with a glass of the traditional Tuscan dessert wine, Vin Santo.

Italian customs can be confusing to North Americans. One sunny day we decided to relax around the pool and maybe go out for lunch. Around 12:30 we decided to drive to Castello di Brolio for lunch, about twenty minutes away.

Me at a Montalcino enoteca.

We arrived to find it's closed on Thursdays. Next we tried Castello di Meleto – closed for siesta. The nearby village of Gaiole offered a choice of restaurants; the first two were full, the third too noisy and smoky. We drove back up a hilltop in one last desperate attempt at lunch ... closed. Defeated, we went to a local store, bought meat and cheese, and returned to the villa for a 3:30 lunch. To complete our frustration, at dinner that night at Casa Mia, both our credit cards were refused, for reasons still unknown. The accommodating owner asked where we were staying and said, "Come back tomorrow and we'll try it again." We returned the next morning with a third credit card and were treated to cappuccinos while we waited. *La dolce vita* at last.

Another great tip the Malones gave us was to visit the sixteenth-century building that houses Dievole winery, about fifteen kilometres north of Siena. They offer regular tours in English, and while we waited, a lovely elderly woman served us a glass of wine, bread, and olive oil, all complimentary. A young male family member led us on a tour of the estate. Each stop featured a different wine and a food accompaniment like pecorino cheese. Even the family chapel was a wine stop where the long history was described; same thing in the barrel cellar, the vineyard, and, finally, the tasting room. There we learned that their Canadian agent was Don Ziraldo, a St. Catharines native and pioneer of Niagara wines. It may have been the best winery tour I've ever been on.

Provence and Southern Rhône

Just say the word, Provence, and hedonism comes to mind: croissants and café au lait, rosé and *jambon* for lunch, *l'heure joyeuse* (actually, they call it happy hour in France), and a sumptuous multi-course dinner. Put on a fire and sip a marc for a *digestif*.

We had rented a villa outside Ménerbes with our friends René and Elaine Bertrand, who had visited Provence a few times before. The villa was lovely, but it was cold; it was the last week of April, and the owner had turned the heat off. It was so cold that a trip to the ceramic tiled bathroom was like going into a meat locker (René claimed after one visit to have two belly buttons). So cold we had to buy a heater for the bathroom and heat the kitchen with the gas stove. Eventually, the landlady relented and turned the heat back on. Nonetheless, she was referred to as *la bitch* for the duration.

We busied ourselves going to outdoor markets to buy fresh produce and meat, which René and Alice would turn into gourmet meals every night. There was a market in every town, each on a different day. There were Roman remains to see in Arles, Orange, and Aix, and fabulous hilltop villages like Gordes, Lacoste, and our own Ménerbes, all with stunning views.

One day we walked into a drab storefront in Ménerbes to have a *pression* (draft beer) at the tiny bar. The madame suggested we go to the back of the store, where we found a balcony. The view of the Provençal countryside was breathtaking, and we returned more than once for beer and pizza just to sit there and gaze.

Most of all there were countless vineyards and wineries that we visited often, some with great loyalty. Our local winery preferences, Royeaux and Citadelle, provided us with not only some wonderful wines for our ever-growing happy-hour habit, but also engaging wine conversations and recommendations on all things Provence.

We had a rosé for lunch every day for two weeks, a magnum on the first day (from Gérard Bertrand, in honour of our friends the Bertrands). This is the law *en Provence, n'est-ce pas?* To celebrate the Bertrands' anniversary, we drank Champagne; Crémant was for everyday celebration. I found the rosés, Viog-

A Provençal lunch with our daily rosé.

niers and a few select Provence reds satisfactory for lunch and happy hour, but we chose more complex, full-bodied Rhône reds for the dinner table.

I had long been a fan of wines from Châteauneuf-du-Pape, and that village was one of our first day trips. A recommended winery was closed, so we randomly picked Cardinalys, an underground cave on the main street. Laurent, the proprietor, warned us he was "high end," and we sat around an ancient wooden table and tasted some fabulous red wines, before lunch. At the end of the tasting, we suggested four wines we would like to purchase, all ranging from 45 to 70 euros. The suave Laurent said, "You mean cases, of course." He expressed more than a little disappointment when we said, "No, bottles."

Over an al fresco lunch in the village square, we began our phone and email pursuit of a private tasting at my favourite southern Rhône winery, Château de Beaucastel, which I consider the benchmark for Rhône wines. They don't have a tasting room, and arranging a meeting would take several tries in French and English and some stretching of my wine-business credentials.

We were eventually rewarded with a 2 pm appointment, several days later. It proved to be the tasting of a lifetime. Beaucastel, although huge, is still a family-run business (*famille* Perrin) and doesn't even have a wine store on premise. Richard, our thirty-something host, gave the four of us a complete tour of the vineyards, production facilities, and cellars. Also a lawyer specializing in French wine law, he was able to explain to me why Coudoulet de Beaucastel is one of

Tasting of a lifetime at Château Beaucastel.

the great wine bargains. Many decades ago, a road was put in, severing Beaucastel's main vineyard. Later it was decided that road would mark the border of Châteauneuf-du-Pape, and any wine produced, even across the road, would be designated a simple Côtes du Rhône. Coudoulet sells for one third the price of the Chât-du-Pape, from the same vineyard!

Eventually, Richard ushered us into an enormous, stately room containing a large table on which sat several bottles. Time to taste.

We started with a rosé that Beaucastel was making for Brad Pitt and Angelina Jolie, who own a vineyard in Provence. One of the Perrin sons met the couple in first-class on a flight to Paris from the United States, and they convinced him that his winery should make what was to be called Cuvée Pink Floyd. It was lovely, as it should be for 18 euros. The next wine was the most stunning white I have ever tasted, Burgundy be damned. It was a nine-year-old 100-percent Roussanne, made in such small quantities that it was sold only to select Parisian restaurants, at 90 euros a bottle. This was followed by several vintages of red Coudoulets and two Chât-du-Papes that were thirteen years apart. I have seldom been so delighted as when I nailed the year of the older vintage. Two hours had gone by and we had been treated like visiting royalty; they now have a life-long customer.

We stopped in a couple of tasting rooms in villages, including Gigondas, on our way home and saw something you would see only in Europe: customers coming in to fill their own large containers from a pump, using what looked like gas station hoses, complete with three different price levels to choose from. After Beaucastel, however, every wine, and its pourer, now seemed pedestrian. We were paying the price for perfection.

Easter weekend in the Finger Lakes

If you live in Southern Ontario, the Finger Lakes are two to three hours away by car. Once you get there, scenery and wineries abound, along with plenty of small-town Americana. Viticulturally, however, I find the region to be a kind of poor man's Niagara. Any wine they make, Niagara does it better – and with a much broader range of vinifera grapes.

Canandaigua is a good place to begin: it's located at the head of the closest lake to the border and is home to the New York Wine and Culinary Center, which features a tasting room where you can try flights of five wines for $6 each. There are five themed flights, and the wineries rotate each month. And you can buy the wines right there – what a concept! This is definitely one area in which New York State is way ahead of Ontario and our restrictive alcohol laws. Niagara cries out for such a facility. Above the Wine and Culinary Center is a bar/restaurant that features local wines by the glass, a lengthy New York State beer list, and entertainment on the weekends. There is also an information area where you can stock up on brochures and maps for the rest of your stay and, of course, a gift shop.

A good place to stay is the nearby Inn on the Lake. It has a very good restaurant with a Wine Spectator Award–winning list and a bar that has entertainment on Friday nights. There are three other dinner spots within walking distance. We chose Doc's, which specialized in seafood and offered Clos du Bois Russian River Chardonnay for $25.

We set out the next day after exploring Canandaigua's main street and city pier, which features Cannery Row–style boathouses, and headed to Geneva, at the north end of Seneca Lake, about twenty-five kilometres away. Belhurst Castle and winery seems to be a must-stop-and-see, so we did. It featured a cozy bar with a beautiful view and an expensive dining room decorated in

Heron Hill makes some of the Finger Lakes' best wines.

"castle" style. The tasting-room wines were mediocre and overpriced, and we left with only pictures.

Fox Run is just down the road, and here we were introduced to the industry discount, which served us well for the duration. If you work in the wine industry (just show a business card), purchases are discounted 20 to 30 percent, and tasting fees are waived. Fox Run confirmed what we had learned the previous day: what Finger Lakes does best is Riesling and Cabernet Franc. Dessert wines, where you can find them, are usually good value.

We continued to work our way down the scenic shoreline of Seneca Lake, with stops at Anthony Road (good late-harvest Vignoles) and Glenora (spectacular view). At Glenora, we bought the $25 Brut, noting that the industry discount pretty much covered the 27 percent exchange between the US and Canadian dollar.

A fortuitous stop was Heron Hill, which we drove a mile past before deciding to turn around and go back. The actual winery is on Keuka Lake, so we had not expected this satellite retail store on Seneca. A woman (with a good mid-afternoon buzz on) at the Wine and Culinary Center in Canandaigua had told us it was her favourite winery, and indeed it was the best tasting we had. Even the reds shone; we purchased a 2004 meritage, yet another Riesling and a late-harvest Vidal that had won a gold medal – but they had dropped the price by $2? Go figure.

Our final stop that day was at Lakewood Vineyards, where we lucked into having one of the owners serve us. The winery has good prices and decent wine, especially the gold-medal-winning Gewürztraminer, which was the wine of the day and would be consumed that night.

From there, we drove to nearby Watkins Glen and checked in to the Harbor Hotel. Our spacious room included a lake view, Easter breakfast, and a flat-screen TV to watch the Masters on.

Right next door was an okay seafood restaurant called the Seneca Harbor Station, where we left a third of a bottle of wine that even the next table wouldn't take – those New York wines can be hit and miss.

As we made our way up the Cayuga Lake shore, we spotted a sign for Simply Red Bistro, which had been recommended to us. The mile-or-so-off-the-road detour was well worth it. The bistro is part of Sheldrake Point Winery, and we were warmly welcomed by Bob Madill, one of Sheldrake's founders, when he saw my Calamus sweater. It turned out that he knows Niagara well and had been to Calamus through a connection with Arthur Harder, Calamus's winemaker. They make lovely wines at Sheldrake. The sold-out bistro suddenly had a cancellation, and we fell heir to a table for a late lunch with a glass of rosé and Pinot Gris that were superb. It was our only winery stop of the day, but we couldn't have done better.

Finger Lakes wine seems to be a long way behind what Niagara has been able to produce, especially the reds – and we tasted several from the excellent 2007 vintage. Even without the exchange and state tax of 8 percent, the value quotient doesn't measure up with Niagara.

The wineries are also full of wines made from or blended with Niagara, Catawba, Delaware, and countless other local grapes that give way to descriptors like "candy-floss finish" – all to be avoided in my opinion. Life's too short and all that.

Find out where the gems are, like Sheldrake and Heron Hill, and seek them out. The Finger Lakes Wine Festival takes place each summer in mid-July in Watkins Glen.

Robbery on the High Seas

Sometimes I wish I didn't like wine so much – especially when held hostage by a company like Norwegian Cruise Line.

In 2009, we took a two-week cruise around South America from Buenos Aires to Santiago. The first stop and shore excursion was a winery in Montevideo,

Uruguay. We paid $280 US for a city tour and lunch and afternoon at the winery. It was a small family winery called Bouza, much the same size and age as Calamus, and we had a pleasant, four-wine lunch. I bought two wines to take back: a Tannat/Tempranillo blend and a white that I planned to drink on our balcony. Norwegian's rules were that if you brought the wine on board for consumption, there was a $15 corkage fee, which I found outrageous, given what we had just paid them for the excursion. So I smuggled the wine onto the ship in a plastic water bottle, which, due to its size, I had to place sideways in our tiny cabin fridge. Of course, when I went to retrieve it later that day, half the contraband liquid lay on the fridge floor, thanks to a faulty closure or closer. Foiled again!

Wine prices on board were stratospheric: at least a 250-percent markup and a $12 per bottle service charge in spite of the fact we were already paying a mandatory $24 per day staff tip. When you added a 27-percent exchange rate, $60 to $70 was not unusual for even a mid-tier wine. To make matters worse, the decent, two-hundred-bottle list included some of my favourites, like Gordon Brothers Merlot from Washington State and Ken Forrester Chenin Blanc,

A winery in Montevideo, Uruguay.

Outdoor tasting bar at Concha y Toro.

so it was hard to refrain. Inexplicably, the list included no Argentine wine, the very country we were sailing around! When we went ashore in Chile, I bought three bottles of the cheapest Chardonnay I could find and meekly paid the $45 tariff. You have to cut back somewhere.

I emailed all these wine complaints to the management and received no reply. I had gone to three sommelier-conducted wine tastings during the cruise, and they were meant to cost $25 each. When our final and staggering bar tab arrived at the end of the two weeks, I saw I had not been charged for the tastings. Coincidental? Perhaps, but I like to think that it was my unspoken compensation.

The first night of the cruise was February 2, 2009. Those of a certain age might know that date was the fiftieth anniversary of the "day the music died." I was watching the Super Bowl in the ship's sports bar, drinking several glasses of wine and chatting to the American couple beside me, who appeared to be about my age. Sometime in the second half, I turned to them and said, "Do you know what happened fifty years ago today?" He took a long drink of his wine and said, "We're from Clear Lake, Iowa, and I visited the crash site with my brother." Another bottle was ordered to honour Buddy, Richie, and the Big Bopper.

On the final day of the cruise, we paid another $300 for a Santiago city tour, lunch, and a tour and tasting at Concha y Toro, Chile's biggest winery.

Normally, that wouldn't sound too appealing; we would be the large bus tour that I always try to avoid at a winery. However, they knew how to do "big," and it turned out to be very memorable, tasting their always dependable and correct wines outside on a lovely sunny day. We were also allowed to keep the large tasting glasses they provided, and purchased wines went directly home – no corkage!

New Zealand revisited

In 2010, Alice and I both took leaves of absence from our jobs to return to my favourite place in the world, New Zealand. The trip would last two months, including a week in Rarotonga in the Cook Islands.

After three days in Auckland, we flew into Queenstown, returning to a beautiful alpine town that's part Banff and part Whistler, with a spectacular view of the lake and the Remarkables, Q'town's signature mountain range. From there, we took an overnight trip to Cromwell, the heart of Central Otago wine country. We went to six wineries and stayed in a lovely B & B – on the lake. The wines were all good, and we stocked up knowing we were headed to more remote places like Milford Sound and Doubtful Sound, but, oh, were they expensive. A good Pinot is $40 or more. There is very little under $25 in the wineries, and that is usually rosé. We were very pleased to have the 22-percent exchange difference. This whole area looks just like the South Okanagan; the B & B could have been in Naramata.

In Cromwell, we went to the Victoria Hotel for dinner, where we ordered two glasses of local Pinot Noir. They served the wine in the smallest glasses I've ever seen, filled to the brim. I almost didn't drink it and began to check before ordering and switch to beer if I saw the offending glasses on another table. These miniscule glasses and the warm temperature at which restaurants serve Pinot there were my bane.

Wouldn't it be nice to have something like Queenstown's New Zealand Wine Experience here in Ontario? You get a smart card when you come in, they have eighty wines arranged by varietal, and offer three sizes of tasting – how civilized. You can then buy bottles of the wines you liked. Our bill after an hour or so of tasting was $25, and we got to sample wines like Felton Road Pinot that we couldn't afford to buy. Q'town and Central Otago are, as a Danish woman we met said, "a place I could live."

On our way into Christchurch, we stopped at three wineries. At the third one, we got the owner, for an hour (no one else came in on a Sunday after-

Tasting Kevin Judd's Greywacke wines.

noon), of Sandihurst, which at the time was making what I thought was some of the best-value Pinot Noir and Riesling in New Zealand. When he launched into a rant about the LCBO, we found we had more in common – except for corks. When he bought the winery five years ago, he went back to cork closures, citing sulphur problems under Stelvin.

After arriving at our spacious flat in Christchurch, the first order of business was to meet our Aussie friend Terry at the Holy Grail sports bar to watch the Super Bowl, Monday at noon. The place was huge and packed. I found a rail table on the third floor and had the perfect neighbour, a thirty-something sales guy with an expense account, who took two days off every year for the Super Bowl: one to watch it, the other to recover. He saw my Canada hat and immediately wanted to know every detail of the 1972 Summit Series between Canada and the USSR. He had come to the right place. By the time his friends (Canadians living in New Zealand) and Terry arrived, he was buying what became an endless round of beers and wine and soon had offered me a private box at the big cricket match the next day. (I had to decline.) The crowd was very pro-Saints and was in a frenzy by the end of the game. We staggered out of the bar into daylight and met Alice, who had been in the library all afternoon in a fruitless search for a long-lost great uncle who had been a local sheep farmer. We rallied for happy hour back at the flat and then hit an Indian BYO with a couple of bottles in hand. It seems we had picked up with Terry where we left off five years earlier in Australia.

Tasting bar at Forrest winery in Marlborough.

A year later, to the week, Terry sent us pictures of the building we had stayed in for four nights, almost completely destroyed by the Christchurch earthquake.

The next afternoon, we did the hour drive up to the Waipara wine area and visited three wineries. We hit another jackpot with the middle one: we had the Torlesse winemaker to ourselves for an hour. After tasting an even dozen, including a Port-style dessert wine, we left with Pinot Gris, Gewürz, and Riesling: aromatic whites is what they do best in Canterbury.

We spent the final day seeing the sights of Christchurch, the South Island's biggest city (population 350,000) and having a fabulous dinner with Susan and Cyril (and offspring), long-time friends of Terry, at their home overlooking the city. One of the many wines brought out was a Greywacke Sauvignon Blanc, by winemaker Kevin Judd. Cyril explained to us that this was the first release by Kevin, who had been Cloudy Bay's winemaker for twenty years and had just parted company the previous year. The kicker was we already had a meeting set up (by Henry of Pelham's Paul Speck) two days hence in Marlborough to taste with Kevin.

Our first day in Marlborough, we met with Kevin at Dog Point (my personal benchmark Kiwi Sauvignon), whose facilities he used to make his wine. We piled in his truck with his dog, Dixie, and he drove us through the vineyards, explaining the nuances of the topography. Every vine is irrigated here, and there is a stark difference between the green vineyards and the brown of all the other vegetation. Back at the winery, we tasted through Kevin's four-wine portfolio; his Sauvignon Blanc and Pinot Noir have since appeared in the LCBO.

This was the weekend of the Marlborough Wine & Food Festival, attended by 8,000 people. We awoke the next day to the realization that the festival was sold out. I had my trade pass, but what of Alice and Terry? We took the shuttle bus out to the site, in a driving rain, the first time that had happened in the event's twenty-eight-year history. I went to the festival office and said I was a visiting journalist. I happened to have my *Vines* story from five years earlier with me, and before you knew it, the three of us were in the sponsors' tent, eating and drinking, the $40 admission forgotten.

We had a great day of music, wine, and revelry before taking the shuttle back to a beer-tasting bar and then enjoyed a superb dinner at Bacchus.

Terry's favourite wine at the Wine & Food Festival had been a Forrest Riesling, so we went to the winery the next morning to buy some (and actually refused all tasting offers). We were met by owner Dr. John Forrest, who had been a medical-school classmate of Susan's. He had built this winery into a 100,000-case business and told us that the 8.5-percent Riesling we had bought was what was "paying the bills" – it's the biggest selling Riesling in New Zealand.

On our second bottle of Alpha Domus Viognier with Bill and Charlie.

Next stop was the mountain town of Nelson. It was Valentine's Day, five weeks on the road, and the halfway point of the trip. We had a lot to celebrate, so we took Kevin's restaurant advice and headed to the Boat Shed Cafe, which was actually just that, made into a high-end eatery. The Nelson area is packed with wineries, and a chance stop at one of them, Seifried, led to hiring a new sales agency at Calamus a couple of months later after they gave us the name of their Ontario agent.

We said goodbye to Terry in Nelson and took the three-hour boat ride to Wellington, at the south tip of the North Island. The next connection was with Bill Pallet, a Ryerson friend, and his partner, Charlie. They were on a cruise and docked in Wellington for the day and had just come from the Olympic opening ceremonies in Vancouver. Over two bottles of Alpha Domus Viognier (best white of the trip), we got a complete recap of the ceremony with pictures. We had missed the whole thing so got quite an emotional tingle having Bill recount it only a couple of days later. Bill and Charlie came very close to missing their boat because of that second bottle of Viognier.

We headed north to Martinborough, a wine village we had visited five years earlier. We had two great tasting experiences at Ata Rangi and Te Kairanga wineries. We returned to a favourite restaurant, Est, and shared an eight-flight wine tasting with our meal, four whites and four Pinot Noirs. It was fabulous and cost the same as one bottle would have.

We had decided we needed a vacation from our vacation: that is, to stay in one place for seven whole days. We couldn't have picked a better place than Te Awanga Cottages, twenty kilometres down the coast from Napier. It had it all, including satellite TV with all seven Olympic channels, which meant we could watch the second week from Vancouver. That also meant seeing the last four hockey games. Oh yes, and there were four wineries and several restaurants nearby. We had dinner at one of the wineries, Elephant Hill, which had cost $50 million to build and was owned by Germans who visited only occasionally. It was also one of the very few wine lists we saw that had wines from all over the world.

The men's gold-medal game began at 9:15 am on Monday. I took off my Leafs T-shirt after regulation time ended, thinking it may be jinxing them, and put on my Canada hat that had been on top of the TV. It worked. After Sid's golden goal, we popped our bottle of Palliser bubbly and then went to one of the nearby wineries for a celebratory lunch. As people were partying in the streets across Canada, 10,000 miles away in New Zealand, it caused nary a ripple.

This area, known as Hawke's Bay, is home to some of New Zealand's best wineries, an almost perfect climate, and engaging topography. If I could move anywhere in the world I've been, it would be here.

A pair of Saltspring Island wines.

British Columbia

My first encounter with a good BC wine was a 1982 Mission Hill Cabernet Sauvignon I had at a tasting somewhere. I was so impressed I ordered a case, which was sent by bus; it was $18 a bottle. The wine was lovely, the case emptied quickly, and I tried not to feel too disappointed when I found out the grapes were from Washington State.

Since 1990, I've gone to BC every four years and have covered most of the viticulture areas of the province; grapes seem to be grown everywhere. On my last visit, I had a lovely white from the Creston Valley, previously known only for apples. At a recent dinner party, I served up an impressive red from Saltspring Island. The little-known and hard-to-pronounce Similkameen Valley is producing some stunning wines and, of course, the various sub-regions of the Okanagan Valley now produce wine rivalling anything in the New World.

After a 1994 trip, I brought back a case of various BC wines for a tasting showdown with Ontario wines from the same grapes. The Noble Rotters were assembled and the blind tasting began. The results after the corks were drawn was a resounding 5–0 victory for BC. I had hoped for a more favourable result, but the palates had spoken.

I became a believer in BC wines from that moment and continue to be impressed with how BC consumers have embraced their local product. The province has its own chain of VQA stores stocking only wines grown and made in BC, and, unlike Toronto, you are hard pressed to find a Vancouver restaurant that doesn't feature local wine. From a golf course in Kaslo to a bar in Tofino, I found a choice of provincial wines that were proudly offered. As the T-shirt says, "Think global, drink local."

Epilogue

One of the conclusions I've come to after all my wine travels is that Canada is a world-class wine producer and should work harder to establish an international reputation for more than Icewine. Yes, we grow too many varieties, definitely have vintage variation, and are entering only our second generation of winemakers. Outside of the southern Okanagan, we cannot produce the kind of jammy, high-alcohol reds that remain popular with consumers, but with some governmental marketing support, Canada could be an international player. Riesling, Cabernet Franc, Chardonnay, Pinot Noir, and sparkling wine will be the vanguard.

New Zealand, with its four million residents and 400 wineries, exports 50 percent of its wine, couldn't be farther away from its foreign markets, and is priced considerably higher than the sea of Australian wine it sits next to. Chilean wines are sold everywhere in the world I've been, and is there any place on the planet you can't buy a California Chardonnay?

Ontario, in particular, has a battle to fight on two fronts: acceptance at home and respect abroad. It may take another generation, but the wines are already good enough to win the fight.

★★★

Of course, we did more in our travels than drink wine and visit wineries, but that was where I met the most interesting people. There seems to be a bond, a certain camaraderie between people who truly appreciate fine wine, whether they work in the business or not. The later experiences were certainly enhanced by the fact that I worked at a winery, that I had my "own" vineyard and some journalistic credentials – before that I got by on "wine knowledge," but more importantly a shared passion with people all over the world. There are many universally shared passions; mine happens to be wine. So I will continue to paddle down life's river, searching for new wine adventures around the next bend.

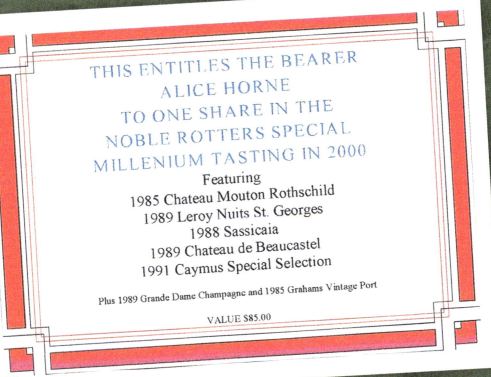

A share certificate for the millennium tasting.

Wine Hall of Fame

The game of naming your favourite bottle is a hopeless task, but it's so much fun trying. There are so many factors: people, place, mood, and ambience, to name a few. Think of all the great wines you leave out. "Best" means selecting only one and usually turns out to mean most memorable. It could also be the bottle you open tonight.

The same applies to all the other "best ofs" in your life, but I will attempt it here in a variety of wine-related categories – my personal wine hall of fame.

Best Restaurant Wine List:
BERN'S STEAK HOUSE, TAMPA, FLORIDA

I was recently given a bound hardcover copy of the list: sixty-five hundred bottles, two hundred by the glass. Seventy-seven pages of French wines alone, many of the older vintages recorked.

Best Restaurant Wine Dinner:
SOOKE HARBOUR HOUSE HOTEL, SOOKE, BC

It helped that we were carrying a bottle of late-harvest Ehrenfelser for the owner from noted chef and author John Bishop, whose restaurant we had dined at the night before.

Best Restaurant Wine Lunch:
LA TABLE DE PIERRE BOURÉE, GEVREY-CHAMBERTIN, BURGUNDY

It's hard to go wrong with any wine from this village, but after enjoying seven different glasses with lunch, you could buy the ones you liked best.

Enjoying a beautiful day at the Marlborough Wine festival.

BEST WINERY TASTING:
Château de Beaucastel, Orange, Southern Rhône

Private tour and tasting for almost two hours, and no store to exit through.

BEST WINERY TOUR:
Dievole, Siena, Italy

I've recommended it to anyone who's going to Tuscany. *La dolce vita*.

BEST OVERALL WINERY EXPERIENCE:
J.B. Becker, Rheingau, Germany

Sometimes you just get lucky and are carrying the right book.

BEST PRIVATE WINE CELLAR VISITED:
A tie:
Larry Malone's in Chicago, René Bertrand's in Toronto

Best Wine Festival or Fair:
MARLBOROUGH WINE & FOOD FESTIVAL, BLENHEIM, NEW ZEALAND

It helps to have VIP status for you and your entourage.

Best Noble Rotter Tasting:
JANUARY 2000 MILLENNIUM TASTING, GRANO RESTAURANT, TORONTO

There were 128 to choose from, many of them stellar, but #72 featured a fifteen-year-old Mouton Rothschild, a Sassicaia, a Beaucastel, a Caymus, a 1989 Nuits-Saint-Georges and an '85 Graham's Port. Not a disappointment among them, including the opener, an '89 Veuve Clicquot La Grande Dame.

Best Non-Winery Tasting:
NICO VAN DUYVENBODE, 1960S AND '70S BURGUNDIES

Nico was an Ottawa-based collector and raconteur who bought up wine cellars from Scottish castles. Some of us regularly tasted these rare wines, usually twenty years and older and always French. Nico didn't like tannin.

Best White Wine:
2002 BEAUCASTEL ROUSSANNE

It was hard to believe that this little-known grape, almost always blended, could produce white wine nirvana.

Best Red Wine:
1997 OPUS ONE

Opulent, silky, decadent, with a finish into next week. I tried a few vintages before the price went into the stratosphere. Plenty of contenders for this crown, but if there can be only one "best," it's Opus.

Alice drinking Champagne at Stormy Weather.

Acknowledgements

My wife, and willing accomplice in wine drinking, was very encouraging and supportive in this project. There is no one I have enjoyed drinking with more than Alice B, and I still make her guess the wine every time. Anytime she thinks I'm being extravagant with a wine purchase, I remind her of the time we walked into a Hong Kong bar called Stormy Weather and she ordered a $100 bottle of Mumm's Champagne, just because she felt like it.

My brother, Robin, who has been with me all the way through this journey, as is well documented in these pages. He's been my partner in wine, music, and anything to do with construction, and I am forever grateful for his camaraderie.

No one has bought more wine from me, both Calamus and Horne Brothers, than my sister, Elizabeth, and the good doctor Levine. No one knows how to celebrate life any better.

Shaun Markey, a friend of forty-five years, was my inspiration for this book, after I read his book on antique collecting. Shaun was also very supportive of my Calamus career and wrote several of the early press releases.

Alice, Dick Singer, and his wife at his Prince Edward County vineyard.

Lesley Fraser, who recently worked on Charles Bronfman's memoir, *Distilled*, for HarperCollins, agreed to be my editor. We have been enjoying wine together for more than twenty years, and she has been crucial to the completion of this project.

Michael Pinkus, wine writer, with whom I have tasted more bad wine (and a few gems) than anyone could imagine.

Pat, Derek, Sheila, and Arthur at Calamus, who built a business from nothing and continue to make that winery the benchmark for good value in one of Niagara's loveliest settings.

Thank you to all the wine writers I have met, especially Bill Munnelly, Rick VanSickle, Zoltan Szabo, and Chris Waters. Also, the late Dick Singer, who shared the same vision of planting vines and making wine in Prince Edward County that I did in Niagara.

To all of my friends who have bought wine from me, keeping me afloat in my second career, thank you!

CPSIA information can be obtained
at www.ICGtesting.com
Printed in the USA
LVOW06s2202290916

506775LV00006B/7/P